Woman
should know
about her partner's
Money

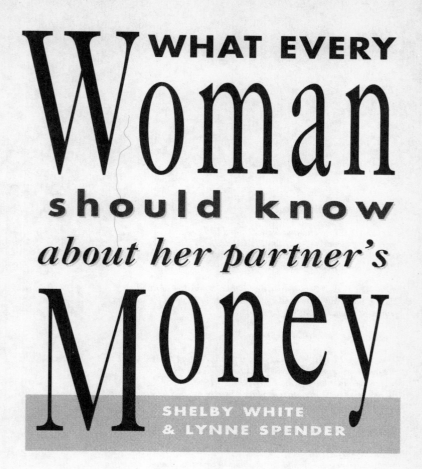

WHAT EVERY Woman should know about her partner's Money

SHELBY WHITE
& LYNNE SPENDER

Hodder & Stoughton
An imprint of Hodder Headline Australia

A Hodder & Stoughton Book

Published in Australia and New Zealand in 1994
by Hodder Headline Australia Pty Limited,
(A member of the Hodder Headline Group)
10-16 South Street, Rydalmere NSW 2116

Published in the US by Turtle Bay Books, a division of Random
House, Inc., New York, and simultaneously in Canada by Random
House of Canada Limited, Toronto.

National Library of Australia Cataloguing-in-Publication data

White, Shelby.
What every woman should know about her partner's money.

Australian edition.
ISBN 0 340 62190 7.

1. Women - Australia - Finance, Personal. 2. Married women -
Australia - Finance, Personal. I. Spender, Lynne. II. White,
Shelby. What every woman should know about her husband's
money. III. Title. IV. Title: What every woman should know about
her husband's money.

332.0240655

Printed in Australia by Griffin Paperbacks, Adelaide

ACKNOWLEDGEMENTS

THANKS TO THE FRIENDS whose stories form the basis of this book. All whom I approached were generous with their time and with their tales, even when the latter showed them in a light that they would have preferred to keep hidden—even from themselves. As always with a book of this nature, there are too many such people to name, but I would like to mention Sarah Neal, researcher extraordinaire, Marion Brown, Sue Deane, Anne Thacker and Keith Wearne. And I must mention my parents, Ivy and Harry Spender, whose lifelong experience as money managers was invaluable.

To Shelby White, who wrote the original *What Every Woman Should Know...* I owe thanks for the enormous amount of work that went into the development of this book. I also owe thanks to Jill Hickson who saw the potential for an Australian version of this book and to Robyn Flemming who edited the book with sensitivity and insight. Philippa Sandall, who nurtured from the sidelines with the sort of sophisticated 'coaching' that many football parents would be advised to emulate, also deserves a special mention.

Finally I wish to thank Dale for the constant inspiration that you can do it all, and Gail, who contributed her legal knowledge and perpetual good humour, enabling me to get it all done.

LYNNE SPENDER

CONTENTS

WHAT EVERY
Woman
should know
about her partner's
Money

MARRIAGE
is not an
EQUAL OPPORTUNITY

'FOR MANY OF US,' says Virginia Dowd, managing director of Australia's Women's Investment Network, 'money is a dark little area of incompetence and the last frontier of self-disclosure.'

Much as we might dislike this image of ourselves as women of the 20th century, Dowd's comments are borne out by statistics, studies and stories. For a variety of reasons, the same modern women who have moved into the work force, and juggle paid work, families and homes, have a dismal record when it comes to financial planning. Money is something we don't talk about—to our partners or each other. And too often it is something that we don't do anything about.

Yet, many women, whether based on a tradition of dependence or the reality of lower wages, have a fear of being financially destitute. Even women with substantial earning ability fear the 'bag lady nightmare'. This is in part because women have no tradition of wealth. A 1980 United Nations' study showed that women own less than 1 per cent of the world's wealth. But it is also in part because what we have is often contingent on our relationships with partners, fathers and male bosses. We know it could easily be taken away.

BREADWINNERS VERSUS BREAD-BAKERS

When it comes to money and marriage, old stereotypes persist. Women have been coming out of the kitchen and going off to work for the past twenty-five years. We have had a sexual revolution, a divorce revolution and a work revolution, but not, yet, a marriage revolution. We have entered into an era of gender neutral language that has attempted to eliminate the sexism in our vocabularies. Our legal system purports to make no distinction between males and females, and our classrooms are enrolling more women than ever in areas previously reserved for males. In the 1960s, male undergraduates far outnumbered female undergraduates in law faculties across Australia. By the 1980s the number of women entering law school exceeded men in several universities.[1] The same trend of increasing numbers of women entering previously male-dominated professions holds for accountancy and medicine.

Despite these changes, the promised equality has not materialised. As Hugh Mackay says '. . . the redefinition of gender roles . . . has taken place in the minds of roughly half the population—the female half'.[2] In terms of the changes that are taking place in gender relations, 'it is still fair to characterise the typical Australian male response as being a dim awareness that something has gone wrong with his life'.[3]

Inside the home, tradition takes root. In the International Year of the Family, we may have blended families and extended families, but we still have families. And in the privacy of our families, *women are not equal*. Women are still 'housewives' taking care of the inside of the house, paying the daily bills and caring for the children. Their partners do the outdoor work. It is interesting to note that gardening (for maintenance, not for pleasure) is one of the few tasks that takes up less time than it did twenty years ago. Almost all of the unpaid work done by women requires more labour now than it did in 1974.[4]

Men and women continue to define their roles in marriage according to traditional tasks. Men think of themselves as the breadwinners. For many men, the primary definition of masculinity is being a good provider for the family. Men still equate money with power and self-esteem, and lots of women agree. Many women connect money with power. In contrast, women think the definition of femininity is being able to balance work and home while caring for people. Men think femininity is being unlike men—presumably without power and money. Even *The Shorter Oxford English Dictionary* defines feminine as 'effeminate'.

For generations, Australian marriages were bound by a legal system that gave power to husbands. Now, the laws have changed. Modern marriage is supposed to be about equals. The problem is, men are resisting the change and continuing to use their higher earnings as a way to control their marriages. Women have adapted to working outside the home, but men have not as easily adapted to having working wives. Men are still reluctant to share the housekeeping. In fact, a study commissioned by the Commonwealth Office of the Status of Women in 1991 found that even when women are in paid work, they still do far more unpaid work than men. Regardless of the number of hours of paid work women do,.they still do twice as many hours of unpaid work as men.[5]

Facts and figures indicate that the more money a man earns, the less willing he is to do the housework. The amount of housework a man is willing to do has little relation with the number of hours his partner works, but instead relates to the amount of money he earns.[6] There is probably nothing quite so annoying as having the debate about responsibility for housework cut short by a male assuming that it can all be solved by having someone come in once a week to clean. The underlying assumption is that the more money you have, the less responsible you have to be for cleaning up your own mess, a sentiment that does not sit easily with Australian ideals of egalitarianism and fair play.

When children come along, traditional roles are further emphasised, as are the differences in the hours that women and men spend working in the home. The Office of the Status of Women's study found that, on average, a new mother's hours of unpaid work increase by 91 per cent, to nearly 56 hours per week.[7]

What is control? How does it work in marriage? Basically, it means that the husband can make decisions to which his wife is afraid to object. As one woman said, 'I was always afraid I would find myself out on the street with three children.' She didn't feel she had any entitlement to make decisions or to object to his decisions, because she didn't earn the money.

Even when women have earned money, leaving the paid work force in order to have children makes them feel vulnerable. In an ironic twist associated with women becoming more equal with their male partners, many report feeling that they are not pulling their weight when they take time out to have children. One went so far as to contribute to a joint account each week from her savings. Her husband felt no such obligation to share the child care and domestic chores on such an equal basis.[8]

Sometimes the control that comes with financial clout is quite subtle. One example is the two-income family where the couple argues about which one of them will pick up the children from school. The one with the lower pay cheque usually picks up the children. The argument appears to be about time and responsibility, but it is really about power and control.

Jenny Prendergast is typical. Initially trained as a biologist, she took on teacher training so that she could spend more time at home when she had children. She and her husband bought a small house in the suburbs. In the three years since their daughter was born, Jenny has continued to work as a casual teacher, on call and out of the promotions running. Her husband Peter's career, at a large corporation, has continued to advance.

Once able to support herself, the arrival of a baby and the costs of running a house have added expenses that Jenny could no longer manage on her own. She has become financially dependent. Her lower earnings have put her in a position in which her husband can use his higher wages as a rationale for handling the assets and otherwise controlling the finances of their marriage. 'I just try not to think about it or I'd be permanently on edge. I do what I have to do each day and assume it will get better when I get back to earning money.'

In other cases, however, control is wielded directly. A typical example would be the man who decides to buy an expensive stereo set even though his partner would prefer that the money be spent on clothes for the children. He earns the money, so he gets to buy the stereo. It is not surprising to discover that the more money the man earns, the more likely it is that he will manage the assets. The only leverage she has, said one non-earning wife, is to withhold sex.

For 'modern' women brought up to think they would be equal financial partners in the marriage, the reality comes as an unpleasant surprise. Frequently there is a big change from before marriage or living together, when each paid their own way. Even while living together, they probably continued to split expenses.

For many women, the arrival of children means a dramatic shift in the balance of their marriages. For one thing, the husband may suddenly see his wife as a 'mother' and want her to assume a more traditional role. Certainly, as Jessie Bernard reported in 1974, women are expected on marriage to become 'neuter'. She points out that in the East European *shetl* this was recognised by a rite of passage, the cutting of a woman's hair— she must no longer attract other men.[9] In my own case, it was expressed in disapproval of clothes worn before marriage that became 'too revealing' after marriage.

Then, too, a wife may discover that she can no longer contribute at the same level financially. This is especially true if she stops working, a decision both make together, but which has a much greater impact on the wife.

UNEQUAL PAY

The equality women thought they would have at work hasn't really happened either. Women as a group are paid less than men. Notice the use of the word 'paid'. Usually headlines read, women continue to 'earn' less than men, making it seem as if women were somehow less deserving than men.

Women are clustered in a relatively small range of occupations in lower paid service and nurturing roles. And many work part-time. This means that in spite of equal pay decisions, women still earn less than 80 cents for every dollar earned by men. Executive women do only 42 per cent as well as executive men. The statistics vary, but rarely do women do better than men.[10]

Women are more likely to interrupt their careers to raise their children. When they do, they often fall behind men in the wage race. Women who go back to work, after they have taken time off, may have to accept a lower paying job or they may lose some superannuation benefits or seniority at their former jobs. And this in spite of maternity leave, the *Sex Discrimination Act* and *Equal Employment Opportunity* legislation.

Many women choose to take less demanding jobs in order to spend more time at home with their children or, increasingly, to care for elderly parents. A growing number are discovering that they must take care of their own elderly parents and their partner's elderly parents as well. An example is women law graduates who settle for lower-level jobs in legal departments of large corporations or the public service, instead of committing themselves to the long and often erratic hours demanded by law firms offering more lucrative partnerships. And such women are frequently paid less than male lawyers in similar jobs.

Women who enter fields formerly reserved for men also often find themselves in the caretaker jobs. More women doctors become general practitioners, the lowest paid field, than brain surgeons, one of the highest paid areas of medicine, which continues to be dominated by men.

Annalyn Swan, editor of *Savvy* magazine, announced in February 1990 that she would leave her job. 'Life has a way of making certain decisions for you,' she told her readers. 'In my case it was the illness of a parent. Faced with the prospect of frequent travel and intensive care, I realised like many other women, just how much our society still depends for care giving on women. For me, at least, the choice was clear. Life became a matter of being not just an editor but more importantly, a daughter.'[11] Swan is 'sequencing', the term sociologists apply to the trading of office jobs for more independent projects. Swan writes that more women will opt to do this. It is hard to imagine reading a 'swan song' like hers from a male editor-in-chief.

THE CHALLENGE to MEN

The income women have been bringing home has been a mixed blessing. While some men welcome the money because it allows them to share responsibility for the family's welfare, and may even allow them to take business risks they might otherwise forego, many men feel threatened when women work and become more independent. And no wonder. Men have a lot to lose. When a wife works, she not only brings home a salary, she also begins to feel independent. Older husbands, especially, may resent their wives' earnings and usurpation of the traditional male role. Perhaps this is because many women work to supplement their partner's income. A study of migrant women workers in Melbourne found that 80 per cent worked not for pleasure but for economic survival. In 14 per cent of cases, they were the sole income earner in the family.[12]

The husband already feels inadequate, since he is not fulfilling his expected role of supporting his family. Many women, capable of earning even more than their partner, sense men's discomfort. They decide they would rather have the marriage than the career, so they pull back. Even young women who have not yet embarked on 'serious' relationships are aware that men and money is a sensitive issue. Renate Klein, coordinator of Women's Studies at Deakin University, Melbourne, reports that her female students are very comfortable with the idea of keeping their own names when they marry, of continuing their careers and maintaining their personal friendships—whether their partner likes their friends or not. But they baulk at keeping their own money. They are distinctly uncomfortable with the idea of both partners putting all their financial cards on the table. Somehow the romantic notions of love and commitment don't sit well with insisting on financial independence. 'I can't do that. He'll think I don't trust him.'

Since in almost 80 per cent of families, the husband is the larger contributor to the family income, the wife's work is deemed less important and less essential. His salary is considered crucial, hers incidental. (Pin money, it seems, came from the association of a wife's earning with something very small and insignificant.) This frequently turns into the 'I can't afford to work' syndrome. And if money is the issue, it's undoubtedly true. After child care, transport, clothing and tax are deducted from the wife's salary, the additional income is too small to warrant the time and effort. If you add to this the pressure on women to stay at home because their partners then receive a dependent spouse rebate on their tax, or because at home they are eligible for a child support allowance, it can be considerable.

Up to two-thirds of a second pay cheque is likely to be spent on child care, household help, clothing, food and work-related expenses. The result—the wife stays home. The husband seldom gives up his job, because he is usually earning more money. Nor is the child care cost considered as coming from the husband's salary.[13] No economic value is given to the wife's unpaid work of running the house, managing the children or arranging the social schedule, even though a salary based on the tasks performed by the wife can add up to well over $80,000 a year.

But in lower income, younger families, when wives discover they are capable of earning a living, and maybe earning more than their partners, it is the wife who becomes dissatisfied and often wants to leave the marriage. Studies by the Institute of Family Studies and by the Australian Bureau of Statistics show that more women than men are the major decision makers in deciding to separate, and more women than men apply for divorce (56 per cent of younger women and 54 per cent of older women, compared with 37 per cent of younger men and 43 per cent of older men).[14] Although there have been studies showing women plunging into poverty immediately after divorce, many women, liberated from the constraints of marriage, actually work harder and earn more than women who remain married. Marriage itself may be a reason for women earning less money.

Sociologists, not surprisingly, have begun to discover a high correlation between women going to work—full-time and part-time—and the divorce rate in America[15] and the same seems true of Australia.

Many women, frustrated by a glass ceiling at the office and dirty glasses in the kitchen, stay home and become as dependent on their partners as the mothers they had vowed not to imitate. But there is a difference. Their mothers expected to stay home; today's women didn't. In the 1990s, women feel dependent if they stay home with their children, but they also feel guilty. On the other hand, women who try to both work and raise children are often too frazzled to do either job well. The wife tends to find herself with two careers, working mother and working woman. Her partner has only his career.

This change to motherhood and lessened earning power frequently leads to a pattern of male domination of the finances within the marriage. Sometimes this change comes about, not because the husband demands it, but because the wife who earns less or who has stayed home to take care of the children feels that she is not entitled to a say in the finances. One woman, now at home caring for children, confided that her partner, sensing her unhappiness at feeling dependent, put money into her savings account every month. She resented his attempt to 'pay' her. Other women find that this is a reasonable solution. But many women report, regardless of how the money is handled within the marriage, that their partners equate earning power with financial control.

Of course, there are still many traditional marriages, where the wife stays at home and the husband works. There are still many husbands who tell their wives, 'If anything ever happens to me, just call the accountant.' Today, however, many women are saying no to this paternalism. While it is easier for the working woman to do this, because she has some economic leverage, the woman who stays home and cares for the children and helps her husband by freeing him from household chores to be able to devote himself to business—even entertaining his clients—also has a right to share in the finances of the marriage, as partner and decision maker.

Sometimes, a wife must take things into her own hands.

One woman borrowed money from a friend to use as a down payment on a house worth $100,000. The real estate agent, a woman, introduced her to a lawyer, also a woman. She was the lawyer's first client. She didn't tell her husband. She used her own credit to obtain a 5.5 per cent mortgage and showed her husband that they would pay less as owners than they did as renters, while also building equity. Her husband was so impressed he urged her to handle all their money.

Obviously, there are some marriages that thrive on the powerful husband, weak and protected wife relationship. One woman confided, 'I always saw my husband as the merchant prince and he always saw me as the student.' When her husband had business losses, neither one of them could discuss it because it would have destroyed the myths each had created about the other.

MONEY TALK

Unfortunately, many couples enter marriage without ever discussing just how they will manage their finances. This phenomenon was addressed in a talk-back program with broadcaster Geraldine Doogue on the A.B.C.'s Radio National on 30 March 1994. Researchers and those who called in talked about what amounted to a silence when it came to discussing money matters. It seems that while couples pool resources, regardless of their individual contributions, attitudes towards money don't matter. But the moment the relationship starts to waver, contributions become very significant. What was previously unproblematic suddenly becomes the source of resentment and conflict. As soon as contributions are made explicit—who puts in what and who spends what—trouble arises. This explains the jolt that many women have when they decide to separate. It may be the first time that they have confronted their own and their partner's real attitudes towards them—and towards money. As Virginia Dowd put it, 'Prior to marriage, a couple rarely discuss money. During marriage they fight about it.'[16]

When people marry, they bring their own attitudes about money with them even if those attitudes don't clearly emerge in the early and romantic days of the partnership. The wife who was brought up in a home where both her parents worked and kept their money separate may feel guilty—or resentful— if her partner pays for her. The wife who was brought up in a more traditional household may feel uncomfortable if her partner doesn't pay for her. The woman who equates money with love may be disappointed if her partner doesn't buy her expensive presents.

Patterns of spending are also usually carried over from our own childhood. Those brought up by thrifty parents often hate to spend money unless they get good value. An example is the wife who hates eating in expensive restaurants. She ruins such occasions because she always looks at the prices and then calculates the cost of the ingredients. Or the husband who refuses to split the bill when they dine out with others, insisting on only paying for what he ate and drank.

The husband who saw his mother struggle after his father died and left the family with little money wants to put all his money into insurance. If he is married to a woman whose family never believed in worrying about that rainy day, conflicts can result.

Conflict over money isn't always about control. You may want to save every penny for a house in five years, while your partner may want to spend more now and buy a less expensive house. You may want to invest in a new business, while your partner may want to support his ailing mother. You may not mind owing money, your partner may hate it. These are legitimate conflicts open to discussion and compromise—and, let's face it, some pretty tense arguments. Control in the marriage is different. It means you may be forced to do things without discussion, without even knowing the facts.

Today, no woman should be ignorant of her partner's finances, or her own. The woman who feels incapable of handling money will find herself vulnerable and controlled. If a woman doesn't share financial decisions, regardless of who earns the money, her partner has the perfect opportunity to assume a dominant role. If you are put in the position of having to ask for money, you give up control, and then money is used as a reward. Do what he likes and he will get you the car you want.

If your partner is reading this book he may be saying to himself, I try and tell her, but every time I start to talk about investments or my will her eyes glaze over. One man solved this by waiting until he and his partner were taking a long car ride so that he knew she couldn't leave; he then explained his business to her.

There are no longer accepted rules in the marriage game. There is no best way to discuss money. Nor is there a best way to manage money. Some couples like to work on the cheque book together. In some homes neither one wants to tackle the chore. The point here is that you have to discuss your plan and reach a joint decision about how you will do it. Who really likes balancing a cheque book anyway? It's not a privilege, it's a responsibility. The same is true for spending and investing your money. And if you are wondering what happens in other families, here is a rough breakdown. Women tend to play a leading role in day-to-day management of household finances but back away from long-term financial planning issues including taxes, insurance and investments.[17] Experts usually give a few rules for managing money:

◆ *Set aside a special time to talk over your finances.*
◆ *Never discuss money when you are having an argument.*

Each couple must make their own way. We start out with a lot of cultural baggage about roles, about power and even about ability. But serious relationships are also about sharing and trust and responsibility. In the past, women knew their role. For women the traditional role has been that of bread-baker, not breadwinner. Women were not supposed to know about money. Geraldine Ferraro was the first woman to run for vice president in the United States as a major party candidate. When her husband was accused of financial wrongdoing, Ms Ferraro, a lawyer and an experienced politician, said she was 'just an Italian housewife': her husband dealt with the money.

Today women and men have to redefine their roles in terms of economic partnership. Instead of staying home, women work and bring home money, in addition to taking care of their families. Even if a woman is not bringing in the same amount, her contributions count. Women must also take part in what was previously the man's domain, the finances. In the 1990s, no woman should be ignorant about money. You are entitled to know how it is earned, how it is spent, how it is invested. Not knowing will leave you vulnerable while you are in a relationship and in trouble when you leave it.

HERE ARE SOME ABSOLUTELY FRIGHTENING STATISTICS YOU SHOULD STUDY NO MATTER HOW LONG YOU HAVE BEEN TOGETHER AND NO MATTER HOW HAPPY YOU ARE...

◆ In 1991 there were 689,000 widows in Australia.

◆ Thirty per cent of all women older than sixty-five in Australia are widows and will probably survive at least fifteen years after their partners die.

◆ Over one-third of all recent first marriages will end in divorce.

◆ More second marriages than first marriages end in divorce.

◆ The remarriage rate for divorced women aged forty-five to sixty-four is only about one-tenth of that for those under twenty-five.

◆ The number of widows in Australia increased 20 percent between 1976 and 1991.

◆ You are 4.5 times more likely to be widowed than your partner is.

◆ Some 72.6 per cent of all nursing home occupants are women. (If he gets sick you will probably take care of him at home; you, however, will probably end up in a nursing home.)

I do, I DO

WOULD YOU BUY A house without reading the contract? Or take a job without knowing what you were expected to do, how many hours you would work, or your salary rate? Probably not. Yet that is what you do when you sign up for marriage.

Australian law recognises three ways of getting married—civil marriage (by a recognised celebrant), religious marriage (within a recognised church) and foreign marriage (conducted outside Australia according to the laws of the country where the marriage takes place). Proof of marriage is provided by a marriage certificate, prepared by the person performing the marriage ceremony.

Marriage certificates say nothing about your rights. Generally it is now the situation that the law regards each partner to a marriage as an individual who can own their own money and property and retain their own name. It is only on the breakdown of marriage that the court looks into the legal interests of the partners in relation to property, children and money. While married, it is up to married partners to decide how they want to run their lives.

WOMEN, MARRIAGE and POWER: a BRIEF HISTORY

The role of the male as the holder of power in a marriage goes back to the ancient Greeks and Romans. Marriage, for the

Greeks, was governed by the need to protect the *oikos*, the family. The bride was given in marriage by her father. She was delivered over to the groom's house like a package. The husband became the keeper of his wife's property. If she died, her sons got her property or it returned to her family. The Romans continued the family tradition. The term they used was *patria potestas*. So powerful was papa, he even had the right to kill his own sons. Women had far lower status, which is not to say that some of them didn't have great influence.

Our word *marriage* comes originally from the Latin *maritus*, which meant provided with a bride. In Roman marriage ceremonies, as depicted on Roman coins, the couples joined their right hands in a ceremony presided over by Concordia, the goddess who symbolised the union of citizens.

When Christianity began to replace the pagan empire, the Roman concept of marriage was simply incorporated into the new rites. But with a slight change. Christ was now seen presiding over the marriage, but the bride and groom no longer clasped hands. For many years the marriage ceremony was performed at the church door, on the grounds that the church itself was deemed too holy to permit the entrance of a woman within its sacred walls at certain periods of her life. In entering marriage, 'the wife was compelled to relinquish her name, her property, the control of her person, her own sacred individuality, and to promise obedience to her husband in all things'.[1]

The traditional Anglo-Saxon wedding didn't do much to change things either, especially when it came to the wife's status. The ceremonial words, often still used today, implied a *giving* of the bride to the husband. The wife and husband were then assumed to be one unit. This identity was further supported by the wife's assumption of her husband's name, an option that fewer young women are today taking on.

Under the English legal system that we inherited, it was

held during the 18th century that 'the very being or legal existence of a woman is suspended during the marriage, or at least is incorporated and consolidated in that of the husband'.[2] Indeed, it was this concept that prompted Beadle, a character in Charles Dickens' *Oliver Twist*, to comment that 'if the law supposes that . . . then the law is an ass'.[3]

There is little doubt that such an idea came from Christianity and was supported by the findings of the courts, science and the religious dogmas of the time. Science and medicine generally regarded women as weaker creatures than men, both physically and intellectually. The scriptures (man-written) dictated that woman was created for man and bound to obey him. And it wasn't just the church that took this dictate seriously. In 1891, for example, when legal action was taken in England against a husband who with his solicitor kidnapped and confined his runaway wife, *The Times* condemned the legal interference as weakening the institution of marriage.[4]

The reality of this for women meant that in the 18th and into the 19th century, a married woman was incapable of owning her own property and of entering contracts; she could not sue or be sued. Nor could a wife sue her husband because, as they were regarded as one legal entity, that would have been like suing herself. She had no rights to the guardianship of her children. Even the money she earned by her own efforts was automatically regarded by the law as belonging to her husband. In the eyes of the law, a married woman was a 'non-person'.[5]

By the middle of the 19th century the situation began to improve for married women, although not without a battle. Small extensions to the rights of women to have separate wages and earnings were made in laws passed in 1870 and 1882. But not until 1935 in England were women 'given' the same rights of ownership as a man. One wonders who it was who took such rights away in the first place—and what effect this has had on attitudes to women and money over the generations. In a 1994 study of the household spending patterns of more than 1000 Australian and New Zealand women, Mattingley & Partners Advertising found a distinct uneasiness in women's attitudes towards money. They found that 85 per cent of women don't know who to trust for financial advice, and 54 per cent of women think that financial institutions don't take them seriously enough.[6] Anna Starkey from the Women's Investment Network thinks that women are more anxious, guilty and depressed about money than are men.[7]

MARRIAGE LAWS TODAY

Today in Australia, New Zealand, the United Kingdom and the United States, married women have the same legal rights as single women or men, although social expectations still impose different sorts of behaviour. Women can enter into contracts and own property. In the past, because women gave up rights, they gained certain protections. Husbands were responsible for their wife's debts before marriage. They were also responsible for 'necessaries'—basic food, clothing, shelter and health care. In exchange, wives became dependent on husbands who were obliged to provide support and maintenance. This is no longer the case. The new legal language talks about spouses and equality. Today, courts have taken the position that both spouses should be jointly held liable for each other's 'necessaries'.

In 1901 the Australian Constitution vested the powers in relation to marriage, divorce, and the custody and guardianship of children with the Commonwealth, but for sixty years the Commonwealth did not use them. They left these matters to be dealt with under state laws. This meant there were six separate systems of family law. When the Commonwealth did decide to exercise its constitutional powers with the *Matrimonial Causes*

Act in 1959 and the Marriage Act in 1961, the main changes concerned the legitimation of children born out of wedlock (they were made legitimate if their parents subsequently married) and the setting up of one legal code throughout Australia in regard to nullity of marriage and to divorce. It also conferred on the courts, in some circumstances, power to deal with maintenance, custody and property settlements.

In 1975, with the Australian Family Law Act, an attempt was made to solve some of the problems still associated with marriage and divorce under the 1959 and 1961 Acts. The main achievements of the 1975 Act were radical changes to the law of divorce (the abolition of fault and the institution of one new ground in the place of fourteen previous grounds of divorce) and the setting up of a new federal court, the Family Law Court of Australia. The one ground for divorce became the 'irretrievable breakdown of marriage', which existed after the parties had lived separately and apart for not less than twelve months. That Act remains in force in Australia, although the Attorney General has recently signalled that it may be due for an overhaul.

Nothing in a marriage contract or our marriage laws spells out a minimum amount of spending money, a minimum sized home, a car, or anything else. Marriage itself gives no rights to a wife or husband to sexual intercourse. In most states, either partner can be convicted for rape in marriage.

There are certain restrictions on who and when you can marry. Girls can marry at sixteen, boys at eighteen. Both must have consent if they are under eighteen. A girl under fourteen and a boy under sixteen cannot legally marry, but girls over fourteen and boys over sixteen can marry if a court gives special permission.

Unlike Cleopatra, you cannot marry your brother or your half-brother. Should you be greedy enough to want two husbands at the same time, the law will say no. Unlike Indiana in the United States where both parties need not be present for the ceremony, you cannot get married over the telephone,

Other than the cost of the licence and any fee for performing the ceremony, there are no financial requirements for marriage. There are also no financial guarantees. Marriage gives you few rights of any kind at all. It is not until you contemplate ending your marriage by divorce that you will discover that you have some very specific rights—and some possible problems.

Don't assume that the law will protect you. For a long time laws were written to protect the family as a single legal entity with the husband as its head. The courts could not easily invade the sanctity of the home. But today the courts allow individual identity even within a marriage. You and your partner have separate rights, such as the right to have credit in your own name. While the laws may govern asset distribution when you die or divorce, no legislation controls finances as long as a marriage is intact. And a wise woman will keep her own money and know a lot about her partner's. The study carried out by Mattingley & Partners Advertising in 1994 showed that 48 per cent of the women interviewed thought that men were hopeless with household money matters.[8] Only a foolish woman would hand over control of her hard-earned money to a 'hopeless' manager, just to preserve an element of romance in the relationship.

In a marriage you are forming a financial partnership. How you handle money and make financial decisions will affect your relationship. The best time to plan what you will do is in the beginning. That is when you will, especially if you are marrying for the first time, have the least amount of money and be most willing to compromise. Knowing what money there is in the partnership and how it is spent can make it far easier in the long term to have and to hold—both your partner and the money that is rightfully yours.

You may, especially if you are starting over, want to make some decisions with the help of a lawyer or financial counsellor. In that case you may want a prenuptial or cohabitation agreement, a development in Australia that looks as though it will receive legal sanction in the near future. This is nothing more than a contract, something a marriage licence doesn't provide.

DE FACTO RELATIONSHIPS

Referred to also as common law marriages, de facto relationships are created when two people live together as husband and wife without having gone through a religious or civil marriage ceremony. Australian law does not recognise homosexual de facto relationships. Most states, however, recognise heterosexual de facto relationships, and some have enacted legislation to cover the rights and interests of de facto partners.

It is now regarded by most Australians as perfectly normal for couples to cohabit (about 50 per cent do) either before they marry, or as an alternative to marriage. Certainly no 'shame' is today attached to couples who live together. Even so, Marion Brown, principal solicitor at the Women's Legal Resources Centre in Sydney, maintains that in New South Wales a woman's rights and interests are better protected under the *Family Law Act* than under the *De Facto Relationships Act*. Under the *Family Law Act*, property settlements recognise women's unpaid work in the home, looking after the house and children. The *Family Law Act* also looks at a woman's capacity to look after herself financially after the relationship ends. It allows compensation for women who have missed opportunities to earn money, promotions and superannuation because they have been 'at work' in the home.

Says Brown, 'If you are going to live with a man on a long-term basis and you intend to buy and develop assets together, your interests are better protected if you marry. If you don't want to get married, at least make sure your name is on the title of any property you contribute to—and keep accurate records of all money you put towards the household or the assets of the relationship. You should also consider entering a cohabitation agreement.'[9]

COHABITATION and
SEPARATION AGREEMENTS

While our legal system strongly upholds the rights of adult people to enter into contracts—and to have them enforced by the courts—the one exception is contracts between those who have intimate sexual relations, whether within or outside marriage. It is surprising, surely, that in the partnership that you are most likely to enter—and with a divorce rate of close to 40 per cent—you cannot set out mutual responsibilities and have the courts uphold them.

In fact, courts for a long time refused to enforce agreements between married couples on the basis of public policy. That policy is something along the lines that to allow partners in a 'married' situation to agree to terms outside those legally sanctioned by family law is to somehow undermine marriage—or to provide benefits to those who are living in sin. This is a traditional view based on the idea that such a contract between unmarried people is based on a promise of unlawful sexual intercourse or prostitution. For married people, any agreement that provides benefits or arrangements not sanctioned by family law will be overridden by the provisions of that law.

In New South Wales under the *De Facto Relationships Act*, unmarried couples can draw up their own contracts for cohabitation and separation. These can cover the financial and property affairs of the partners. They can be made in contemplation of the relationship beginning, or at any time during the relationship. Agreements typically cover how expenses are to be shared, how property is to be treated, and debts.

Unromantic as it may seem, cohabitation and separation agreements can be beneficial. Not only do they provide the terms on which you live together—and part; they also oblige the partners to turn their minds to the sorts of financial and property issues that married people often ignore—until it is too late.

These agreements do not automatically override the court's jurisdiction to make property or maintenance orders under the *De Facto Relationships Act.* The court and the partners will only be bound by the agreement where it is in writing, signed by the partners, and each partner has received independent legal advice from a solicitor and *has a certificate from the solicitor to this effect.* The certificate has to be in a particular form and has to state that each has been advised of their situation in relation to the agreement, i.e. whether it is to their advantage or not to sign the agreement, which should be fair and reasonable in the light of foreseeable future circumstances. If any of these preconditions is not met, the court can override the agreement.

Cohabitation agreements drawn up by married people can always be reviewed and altered by the court, which can change the agreement if it is unfair. If a partner dies, the terms of the agreement can be enforced against the partner's estate, but any form of periodic maintenance ceases unless the agreement specifically states otherwise.

If you are living together, you can resist the traditional roles of 'husband and wife' in arranging your finances. Keeping your own financial identity can play a role in keeping your individuality. If you are married, knowing your rights may help you to overcome the feeling that many women have of not being confident about participating in financial decisions. This is especially important for women who are in long marriages,

SAMPLE COHABITATION AGREEMENT

THIS AGREEMENT is made on the ...day of .....19....
BETWEEN.................... of ....(the first party)
AND........................ of ....(the second party)
WHEREAS the parties intend to live together.
The parties enter into an agreement which they
intend to be legally binding on them.
IT IS AGREED that the parties shall live together for
an indefinite period on the following terms:

1. The parties agree they shall have equal interests in any
    premises occupied by them as their home and shall hold
    any such property as joint tenants.
2. The parties agree that any property owned separately by
    them before they began to live together shall remain
    their separate property unless such property is the
    family home in which case Clause 1 applies. Property
    owned jointly by them before or subsequent to this
    agreement shall remain their joint property and any
    proceeds of the sale of such property shall belong to
    them in equal shares.
3. The parties agree that while they both maintain
    separate bank accounts and credit accounts the money
    involved in each account shall be the responsibility of
    and belong to the party in whose name it is listed.
4. Any money in joint bank accounts shall belong to both
    partners in equal shares.
5. In the event of one partner relinquishing full-time
    employment because of the birth of children or the
    responsibilities of caring for children, half the money
    earned by the employed partner shall belong to the
    other.

6. The parties agree that each shall be responsible for the common expenses of the family home (mortgage, rates, electricity, phone, etc.) and the expenses of maintaining the children in proportion to their respective incomes.

7. Either party may terminate this agreement with three months notice. Notice is to be in writing. Alternatively this agreement lapses without notice if the parties cease to live together for a period of more than three months.

8. In the event that this agreement is terminated, the parties agree:

   (i) property and chattels referred to in Clauses 1, 2 and 3 as joint property shall be equally divided, or if agreement cannot be reached as to equal division shall be sold and the proceeds of their sale be divided equally between them;

   (ii) if there are children of the relationship, the sale of the home and joint property shall be postponed for a reasonable time and the person caring for the children shall remain with the children in the family home unless further agreement to the contrary is reached between the parties.

9. The parties shall continue to maintain any children of the relationship on the basis of one-fifth of their respective incomes (after tax) until that child reaches the age of 18 or completes full-time education.

SIGNED BY ....
in the presence of ....

SIGNED BY ....
in the presence of ....

Source: Adapted from *The Cohabitation Handbook*, Pluto Press, 1984, p. 191.

have never worked, and have been financially dependent on their husbands. You have rights, and you have a right to know about them and about your share of the family money. While there is no one way to handle the marital finances, there are a few things you might want to consider.

TEN FINANCIAL RULES FOR STARTING A PERMANENT RELATIONSHIP

1   Show him your finances. Naturally you'll expect to see his.

2   Don't forget to find out about his debts. In any partnership business deal, it is the least you would want to know. Belinda Hartnet fell madly in love with a fellow student at university. She finished her studies two years before he did, and they lived together with her working and paying all the bills. When he finished studying, they married with the idea that he would work and pay the bills for a few years; they would have children straight away, while they were young. Then Belinda would return to work. What her husband did not tell her was that he still owed thousands of dollars on his Higher Education Contribution Scheme loan, and instead of having his salary to live on they were facing years of paying back the money. Not surprisingly, Belinda felt this was unfair. Two years later, they are still paying back the loan. They don't have children and have no chance yet of putting anything towards a house.

3   Decide whether you want to pool your assets. This is highly recommended for first marriages, but is not always the best approach for de facto couples. Either way, be clear about how and why you arrange the finances.

4   Decide who will pay for what and how. When one of you makes much more than the other, you may not be able to split expenses down the middle. Some decide on a percentage of their income for common expenses. One couple, where the woman had more money than the man, agreed that she would pay for certain things, but he didn't feel comfortable if she paid in public. They arranged that he always paid when they went out, and that she reimbursed him later.

5. When only one of you earns the money, that one should not necessarily make all the decisions. Financial decisions should be joint.

6. No matter how you split expenses and who earns what, make sure you each have some discretionary funds. One woman, Karen, had always managed her own finances. When she married, she and her partner decided on a joint cheque account. Everything went into it. However, she hated having her partner know and question every expense. The classic answer to objections to discretionary funds is to claim that you want money to buy presents, especially for his birthday and Christmas.

7. If you have separate property, think very carefully about whether you want to put it in a joint account. It's easy to give up control to show that you 'trust' somebody. But you may regret it in the future. There is nothing wrong with having your own money. It is no longer 'unfeminine' to be smart about money matters.

8. Be involved in preparing his tax return as well as your own, and ask questions. Don't worry about sounding ignorant. How else will you learn? You should speak to the accountant, too. Local adult education institutions often have courses on money management. The Australian Stock Exchange and the Securities Institute of Australia both run courses on investment and the stock market.

9. Never sign a contract that you don't understand. Never become a silent partner in his business deals. If you are a director of a business, remember that you can be held accountable for its debts. Insist that you know what is happening before you sign anything.

10. Keep records of *everything*. (See Chapter 3 for details on what to keep.)

MARRIAGE, INC.

I REMEMBER THREE YEARS into marriage explaining to my sister, in what can only be described as ignorant complacency, how my 'late' husband (he was never on time) and I never, ever, fought over money. After marriage we both worked, with me, as a school teacher, earning a bit more than he did. He paid off the mortgage; I paid the household expenses. He had records of the payments; I had no records. Five years later, after two children and a stint of me not working, I turned up on my sister's doorstep distraught. 'We seem to do nothing but argue over money!' She had the grace not to say, 'I told you so.'

What happened to me isn't unusual. Any woman married today is likely to fall victim to one of the Three Ds—Death, Divorce or other Disasters. If you are married now, your odds of ending up alone are high. It is predicted that about one-third of first marriages in the 1990s will end in divorce. For second marriages, the rate is higher.[1]

Recently, my friend Sue, an editor, became suspicious that her husband of twenty years was planning to leave her. Before she could be sure, he had already spirited much of what she thought of as the family assets out of their joint bank account. Although Sue had signed tax returns as a director of her husband's company, she had no idea exactly how much money he made each year from his two pharmacies. Nor, to be perfectly fair, did she know how much money she spent. She didn't have a clue about the family finances.

Even if she never thought about divorce, she should have

known about the money that was coming in and going out. Looking back, she muses that one of the problems of the marriage was her refusal to make any connections between what each of them spent and earned. She also shudders when she thinks of her cavalier attitude towards being a director of the company.

When it comes to knowing about the family money, most women probably fall somewhere between those who know nothing and those who handle all the family finances. Some of us may know our partner's salary, but not realise how much he has put into his superannuation; others may know all about the investments, but not be aware of what extras are included in his salary package.

While researching this book, I discussed this problem with a friend who told me she had thought she knew how much her partner earned, since he gave her his wages each fortnight to manage. One day, however, she saw his pay slip and realised that he was pocketing (or putting away) almost $200 each week.

FIVE THINGS WOMEN DON'T USUALLY KNOW ABOUT THEIR PARTNER'S MONEY

Some or all of the following items may apply to you.

1. How much he earns and how much he owes.
2. How the assets are held (savings accounts, property, shares, etc.).
3. How much insurance and superannuation he has and what kind.
4. How much he spends.
5. How he intends to leave it (the will).

Basically, there are two ways to discover the facts about your partner's finances. The good way is by discussing financial matters throughout the marriage. The other, and less pleasant, way is when financial disaster strikes and you discover you are in debt, that your investments are worthless, or even that you are facing bankruptcy.

Studies show that women tend to abdicate from making investment decisions, even when they manage the household finances. They are either afraid to do so, or think it somehow 'unsexy'. This is probably one of the biggest money mistakes a woman can make. There is no evidence that men are biologically better at managing money—although most of them have more experience. Even if you have no experience in looking after money, you can learn. Take a course, read, and rely on your own common sense. Most of the time you will do as well as your husband—and probably better. There is truth in the old husband's tale that managing a household gives you all the skills you need to budget and make sensible money decisions.

Of course, some women never find out about the facts of their husband's finances until the marriage dissolves tragically through death or divorce. One woman I know had played it 'feminine' and asked no questions about money, allowing her husband to be manly and to handle all the finances. This worked quite well until he told her he was leaving. One of the reasons he gave was that he had met someone who was more sophisticated than she—someone who fascinated him because she was independent and knew about money!

Mary Elizabeth Murray, a retired public servant in the United States, also learned the hard way. When her husband, who had managed the investments, died, Ms Murray let a broker handle her account. Before long, she had lost US$125,000. Without consulting her, the broker had sold her blue chip securities and bought risky investments. Ms Murray took her case to arbitration and was awarded US$419,460. But it was a painful way to learn about investing.[2]

One of the best ways to begin learning about your partner's money, as well as your own, is to think of your family as a small corporation. This doesn't mean that you have to have millions in the bank. It is merely a way of looking at what you do have.

HOW TO CALCULATE YOUR NET WORTH* EVEN WHEN YOU THINK YOU HAVE NO ASSETS

Assets	VALUE
• Home—furniture and household equipment (don't forget such things as a wine collection, a library of books or CD's, etc.)	$
• Superannuation and life insurance policies	$
• Shares	$
• Bonds	$
• Bank, building society and credit union cheque and savings accounts	$
• Money market funds, cash deposits	$
• Land	$
• Business or farm	$
• Hidden assets, such as stock options	$
• Possible inheritance	$
TOTAL	$
Liabilities	
• Outstanding taxes	$
• Real estate mortgages	$
• Loans—personal, home equity	$
• Credit card debt	$
• Car loan	$
• Instalment debt	$
• Business loans	$
• Margin debt on stock brokerage accounts	$
TOTAL	$
BALANCE	$

* Your net worth is the difference between your assets and your liabilities.

If the amount of cash coming in and the amount of cash going out are not equal, and the outgoings are greater than the income, you are spending too much.

Corporations, large and small, generally prepare two types of reports. One is a net worth statement, the other a cash flow statement. Your net worth is really a balance sheet, recording what you have and what you owe, your assets and liabilities on a particular day. Corporations usually do an annual net worth report (profit and loss account), but asset values such as stock

WHAT YOU SHOULD KNOW ABOUT YOUR EXPENSES	MONTHLY EXPENDITURE
◆ Housing—mortgage and rent, household repairs, rates and land taxes	$
◆ Debt service on credit cards and loans, other bank charges	$
◆ Utilities—fuel, gas, electricity, telephone	$
◆ Food and alcohol	$
◆ Personal care—hairdresser, health club	$
◆ Clothing—purchase, laundry, dry cleaning	$
◆ Car—petrol, repairs, insurance, car payments	$
◆ Insurance—life, personal and real property, fire, theft and liability, medical–dental, disability	$
◆ Superannuation	$
◆ Travel and entertainment—non-reimbursed expenses, reimbursed expenses	$
◆ Holidays	$
◆ Children—education, child care, clothing	$
◆ Charity and donations—religious, alumnae associations, health organisations	$
◆ Subscriptions—theatre, magazines, journals, organisations	$
◆ Savings and investments	$
◆ Miscellaneous—cigarettes, lunches, newspapers and magazines, cosmetics—and don't forget vet bills for the cat, the dog and the budgie	$
◆ Child support	$

prices can change quickly, so the net worth is as of the day it is prepared. The cash flow statement lets you see how much money is coming in every month or year and how much is going out—in other words, income and expenses.

Start by looking at what you have. If you and your partner pool everything, you only need one statement, but you should include in your list how each asset is owned. If you have separate assets, you may want to have separate accounts. If you don't want to approach your partner, do it on your own—at least it's a beginning.

WHAT YOU SHOULD KNOW ABOUT YOUR INCOME	
	MONTHLY INCOME
◆ Salary	$
◆ Bonus	$
◆ Interest and dividends	$
◆ Partnership interest	$
◆ Rental income	$
◆ Savings accounts	$
◆ Money market funds	$
◆ Cash deposits	$
◆ Child support	$

Remember: A net worth statement tells you what you have. A cash flow statement tells you what comes in and where it goes.

The list of expenses seems exhaustive, yet there are probably other categories of regular expenditures that you might add when you do a personal list. This list also assumes that you already have all the basics—furniture and electrical appliances. But these days, if you have to set up a new household, the cost of even small items like mops, brooms and garbage bins can add up.

I have avoided using the word 'budget' here, because it is a little like using the word 'diet'—you seldom stick to it.

The amount of money you and your partner spend is extremely important. Yet, we go into marriage—or for that matter, live on our own—with few rules about spending. Ask your friends how accurately they could assess their assets or net worth just off the top of their heads.

The marriage in the following example nearly broke up because the husband and wife could not agree about their spending. Caroline and Michael are like many couples: Michael paid most of the bills, and Caroline had a cheque account to cover everyday expenses. They shared a credit card. One day Caroline noticed the credit card statement on Michael's desk. To her horror, she discovered that he had taken out a credit card loan. When Michael came home that evening she asked him about the loan. In the argument that ensued, Caroline discovered that she and Michael had been living way over their incomes. She even feared they could be bankrupt if they had any unexpected expenses.

Michael thought Caroline was over-reacting. After all, he explained, everything worked out perfectly when he ran the numbers through his computer. Michael had always waved a spreadsheet at her and told her not to worry. This time was different. After years of being intimidated by the authority that the spreadsheet seemed to represent, Caroline demanded an accounting that she could understand. With a pencil and paper. Michael had used the computer as a way to control their finances. Caroline's fear of being in debt finally overcame her fear of challenging Michael and the computer.

When Caroline began going over their expenses she realised that Michael had developed a pattern of overspending. Each year he paid off the previous year's debts with his year end bonus, but somehow the debts were never totally wiped out. They never started the year with a clean slate. With Michael's company in financial trouble, there was a good chance that he wouldn't even get a bonus in future.

Caroline took over the finances. She cut their expenses to the bone, putting them both on a food and clothing allowance. Gradually, over a six-month period, she began to both cut their debt and also their tendency to overspend. Michael admits that for the first time he no longer feels out of control. They are still vulnerable if a major disaster should hit them, such as needing a new roof for the house or a new car, but Caroline thinks they are on the right track.

The problem Caroline faced is not unusual. As in most of what we do in marriage, there are few guidelines. Spending just seems to happen. But it is possible to establish some personal guidelines for the marital finances.

HOW MUCH can YOU AFFORD?

It's easy to figure out how much to spend. You just have to know that you can't pay out more than the amount that comes in. The trouble is, credit. We can always buy just a little more than we can actually pay for, thanks to those little plastic credit cards. Problems develop, however, when you find yourself charging on three or four cards; no one card will get you in trouble, but together they can begin to make a big dent in your monthly expenses. Add that to mortgages and car loans, and pretty soon you could be like Caroline's husband, Michael— totally out of control, but under the illusion that everything is all right because you've put all the numbers through your computer.

Some guidelines follow. If Caroline had known these figures she might have had the courage to stop Michael before a problem arose. While most families have slightly different needs at different times, you might want to compare your family spending with other Australian families.[3]

AVERAGE BREAKDOWN OF EXPENSES

Expenses	PERCENTAGE OF TOTAL EXPENSES (%)
Food	15
◆ at home	8.5
◆ away from home	6.5
Housing	30
Clothing, services	6
Transportation	20
◆ vehicles	8
◆ petrol	8
◆ other transportation	4
Health care	5
Personal insurance and superannuation	8
Other—liquor, entertainment personal care, cash contributions, education, etc.	16
TOTAL	100%

But Caroline needed to know more than their average expenses. She should also have known how much debt is considered tolerable. Even though Caroline thought the only good debt was one that has been paid, Michael was right to borrow money. It's one way to build assets. The problem with Michael's borrowing was that it was going more to luxury goods—fancy restaurants, and expensive suits and holidays—than it was towards building assets.

A reasonable amount of debt for a family is usually considered no more than 35 per cent of your gross monthly income. Of this, you can usually plan to spend around 25 per cent for mortgage and housing expenses. Financial counsellors recommend, if possible, that you have enough liquid assets for three to six months of living expenses.

There are several computer programs that can help you to

keep track of all this information, but all you really need is a pencil and paper. You don't even need a calculator.

One of the most important reasons for knowing all the facts and figures is that this will tell you what you will need if something happens to your partner. If you were left alone because of divorce or death, how would you manage? If you don't know now, you will really have problems later on.

SHARING INCOME, EXPENSES and DEBTS

Not knowing about your joint finances leaves you out of control of the situation. Yet, many women simply let their partners take over. Sometimes women do this because it's easier, because taking charge means they have to take responsibility. Sometimes women let their partners take over because they feel they do not have the right to participate, as they do not earn the money. Yet, in most cases, sharing the financial burden, either because you each earn some of the money or because you both decide and are responsible for the way money is spent, can improve relationships.

There are two kinds of money in a relationship: the money that you and your partner earn and spend, and the investments or other assets that you both own and manage. You have to decide how you want to own and share your income and assets.

There really isn't a best way to own assets or spend money. A lawyer who has seen many couples argue viciously about money during a divorce might advocate separate ownership of all property. A psychologist who has seen couples argue heatedly about money during their marriage might say that unless the assets are merged, there will never be a true marriage.

At different times in your life you may want to do things differently. When Shelby White, the co-author of this book, married her first husband, they had few assets. They each earned a small salary, although his was much higher than hers. They shared everything. They owned their house jointly and pooled their income. When Shelby married for the second time, she had a child from her first marriage and elderly parents. Her new husband had his own family obligations. They also each had separate property. As a result, they have a much more complicated financial arrangement than in their first marriages. As in most second marriages, not all of their expenses are joint.

Who actually writes the rent cheque or manages the stock portfolio may not be important. But you should both know what is going on. Most young couples in first marriages will probably share everything. That is one of the main reasons they get married—so joint ownership is the most logical arrangement, regardless of who earns what. If you both work, you can share major expenses and savings, and each keep some separate money for your own expenses. One of you can keep the cheque book and be responsible for paying the bills—and it is a responsibility and a lot of work—or you can agree to do it together. What you can't afford to do is abdicate responsibility for knowing about your joint finances.

If you do not have a credit card in your own name, but have a card jointly with your partner, you can have your credit report in both names. You must request this when you apply for the card. In this way, you will begin establishing your own credit history. If your account is old, you may have to write to the company to request a change in the way your credit is reported.

If you have your own credit history, you can more easily get a credit card in your own name, should you want one.

If you are widowed and do not have earned income, obtaining a credit card can be difficult. You are better off having your own card from the beginning.

If you have charge accounts in your partner's name, you can

continue using them after he dies, providing you pay the bills on time. But you will probably feel more secure if you change them to your own name.

If you are only authorised to sign your partner's credit card, he can easily cancel it if you divorce. One woman told of being totally humiliated in the small town where she lived when she went to use the account at a local store and was told her husband had closed the account.

If you have a joint cheque account, you should have a separate account as well. If your partner dies, a joint account might be frozen and you would have no immediate cash. If you separate or divorce, you would not be the first woman to find out that your partner cleaned out the joint account before he left. In fact, in a study carried out by the Australian Institute of Family Studies in the 1980s, in 30 per cent of cases one partner took all the money from the joint accounts without any discussion or agreement. You might believe you are one of the civilised 70 per cent, but it's a hard way to find out if you're not.

As mentioned in Chapter 1, a wife used to be able to use her husband's credit to obtain 'necessaries'. This is probably no longer the case, as the *Family Law Act* now covers such situations through spouse maintenance. And a debt incurred by your partner is not necessarily yours just because you are married. You can only be liable for another person's credit commitments in the following cases:

◆ *If you signed an agreement as a co-borrower.*
◆ *Agreed to be a guarantor.*
◆ *If you allowed your partner to act as your agent.*
◆ *If you have made out a power of attorney allowing your partner to sign on your behalf.*

If your husband is a bad credit risk, you definitely want your own credit cards, not a joint account.

STDs — SEXUALLY
TRANSMITTED DEBTS

This phrase was cleverly coined a few years ago to name a phenomenon that was becoming increasingly apparent to financial counsellors and lawyers in community legal centres. A corollary perhaps of the increasing credit status of women in the past decades, women have been signing up as guarantors and co-borrowers for loans taken out by their sons, partners and lovers. And they are the ones ending up in financial strife, even bankruptcy.

It's not difficult to picture how this happens. An innocent—or not so innocent—request from a partner to add a signature to a document. Or pressure to sign a document couched in legalese that even lawyers find obscure. It might be for something as small as a new car or as large as a loan to support a business. One reported case refers to a $2 million debt incurred with the collapse of a former husband's business. If you have signed and he defaults, you can be liable for the whole amount.

Advice from the Women's Legal Resource Centre in New South Wales is that you never sign anything if you don't understand it. And never sign anything 'jointly' unless the benefits are for you as well—and the risk is worth taking. It is not a sign of weakness to take such documents to a financial counsellor or adviser. All good business operators seek advice.

While the law will sometimes step in and release a person who has signed an agreement without knowing its full details, there are many cases where the courts have refused to do so. In one case, a husband obtained consent from his wife to sign a mortgage over her house to guarantee the purchase of a farm. When the agreement was challenged, the High Court did not accept that the wife did not fully understand the consequences of signing. Because the lender's solicitor saw and dealt with the husband and wife together, and the guarantee was signed by the wife in the presence of all parties, the High Court held that the wife was bound to the guarantee *even though the solicitor at no time explained matters directly or personally to the wife.*

KEEPING TRACK

KEEPING TRACK OF RECORDS

Keep the following information on a single sheet of paper
- Tax file numbers.
- Bank account numbers.
- Brokerage account numbers.
- Credit card numbers (handy if you lose your wallet or have it stolen).

Keep the following in a special drawer
- Tax returns for the last seven years.
- Brokerage account statements. (I keep the monthly statements for the current year and the yearly statements for the past seven years.)
- Bank statements.
- Insurance policies:
  ~ Homeowners insurance
  ~ Car insurance
  ~ Life insurance.

Keep the following in a safety deposit box with your solicitor or at your bank
- Title deeds to the house or unit.
- Car registration.
- IOUs.
- Marriage licence.
- Divorce papers.
- Wills.
- Leases.
- Share certificates.

Keeping track of your finances can become a burden and may even get out of control. Keep all the documents that accumulate—for some reason, these multiply when you are married—in a special place. One of you should be in charge of keeping the records. If you have a computer at home, some of the information can be kept that way, but only if both of you know how to use it. One woman admitted that her partner kept all the family records on their home computer, but she had no idea of anything, because she couldn't use the computer. If she needed information, she had to ask her partner to retrieve it.

MONEY MISTAKES WOMEN MAKE

While there are no rules for deciding how you and your partner should divide your money, many women who entered marriage thinking they would somehow work out the money, without talking about it, discovered years later that they had made some terrible money mistakes. Here are some common ones:

1 *Putting inherited money or property in a joint account*
Recently, a friend's daughter married. As a wedding gift, her parents gave the couple a house. But the daughter's new husband had been married before and his first wife used his half ownership of the house as an excuse to claim more maintenance from him. If the house had been kept in the daughter's name, this would have been more difficult.

2 *Using her money for expenses, while her husband's investments increase*
For nine of the thirteen years of her marriage, Helena out earned her husband. They split expenses and used her extra earnings to pay for immediate expenses. This sounds reasonable. But all the time they were using her money, his separate investment account, which he had before they married, continued to grow.

3 ***Signing documents without knowing what they are***
Sue continued to sign documents relating to her husband's business without ever checking what they were. When they divorced, she realised she had been signing away her dividends as a director which he had been using for his own purposes.

4 ***Not getting professional advice soon enough***
By the time money problems become an issue, one partner can hide assets and set up corporations that even lawyers are unable to find.

5 ***Giving up control over her money to show faith and bolster her husband's ego***
Diane's husband took charge of the family finances, mainly her salary, while she worked and he stayed home. Too late, she discovered that he had put them in debt, and she was stuck for the loans. Sue signed everything her husband put in front of her without ever asking what she was signing. As a director of the company, she could have been held personally liable for its debts. As it was, she had no idea what she was signing and in fact had signed away her director's fees for many years.

6 ***Letting one partner keep all the family records***
When they divorced, Elaine didn't have access to any of the records and did not have the money to find out what there was, where it was or how much it was worth.

7 ***Trying to pay an equal share when she couldn't really afford to do so***
Esther's husband had a lot more money than she did, yet they agreed to split everything. Problems developed when she lost her high-paying job and dipped into her savings to keep up her commitments. She spent all her money, and because it was a second marriage had little to leave for her children from her first marriage.

8 ***Using her money to buy something in their joint names while he holds on to his separate investments***
When they split, Abby's husband got half the joint property, but she got none of his separate investments.

9 ***Not keeping records or receipts—especially for cash payments***
Gwen's husband was keeping some of his income hidden. She couldn't prove this, and when they divorced she received a settlement based on his understated tax returns.

10 **The biggest mistake of all—thinking that talking about money is not romantic**
The very processes that would help you at the time of a divorce, or the death of your husband—prenuptial agreements, accurate records about property, knowing the value of stock options etc.—are viewed as unromantic. Not talking about money could lead to most of the above problems.

While many problems lead to divorce, they are often problems that, handled differently, might have been resolved. In Diane's case, her husband got them into debt. Had they made joint decisions, they would probably still be married. But she began to lose faith in him when she saw how he handled what she had always thought of as 'their' money.

The friend who paid an equal share of the expenses, even though her husband was much better off than she, began to resent every cent she had to give him. And, frequently it *was* cents. When they went on a trip he would record even bus fares in his little book. The final rupture came when he suggested that they invite her mother for dinner and then suggested she pay her mother's share of the bill.

A possible divorce is not the only reason you should know about money—how it is spent, where it is kept, how it is invested and how it is owed. It is equally important if you are widowed. Otherwise you will become a victim of what is called 'widowitis'. Its chief symptom is the fear that comes from not knowing what you can afford to do when you are on your own and not knowing how to do it.

But even more important, not knowing about the family finances can leave you in a relationship in which you do not play an equal role in the decision making. It can leave you feeling dependent and vulnerable. Knowing about the assets, keeping the records and jointly making decisions are all part of the economic partnership that the modern marriage is supposed to be. It is not sexy to be 'feminine' when it means being vulnerable and financially ignorant.

FOUR

'JUST sign HERE, DEAR'

WHEN THE HISTORY OF New York in the 1980s is written, Donald and Ivana Trump will loom large as the quintessential twosome. She, a ravishing blonde from Czechoslovakia, who wore beautiful clothes; he, a tall, brash real estate developer who owned hotels and gambling casinos. Magazines fed the public a continuous diet of the Trump style. We saw their glittering triplex apartment, their 250-foot yacht and their palatial Palm Beach mansion. We knew their charities and their friends. We saw their helicopter whisking them to fabulous parties. What we didn't see was a young blonde waiting in the wings. When the papers broke the news of the Trumps' marital split, the banner headlines dwarfed those given to African leader Nelson Mandela, released after twenty years in prison.

While much was made of Mr Trump's liaison with another woman, the main focus of the press was the revelation of the couple's premarital agreement. Details were quickly leaked, alleging that Mrs Trump was to receive US$25 million, their 45-room Connecticut mansion and custody of the children. Various sources further disclosed that the agreement written at the time of their marriage had since been revised three times. His lawyers declared the agreement 'ironclad'. Her lawyers called it 'unconscionable' and 'fraudulent'. Marital behaviour that might have caused Mr Trump to relinquish a large part of his fortune in the past was of no consequence. What counted was the premarital contract. In the end, you could not feel sorry for Ivana. She walked away with US$10 million, the Connecticut mansion, a New York apartment and use of the couple's 118-room Mar-A-Lago mansion in Florida for one month a year, as well as US$650,000 a year in alimony and child support.

HISTORY of PRENUPTIAL AGREEMENTS

Prenuptial agreements have been around for a long time. The Babylonians had them in the first millennium BC. The agreements spelt out the dowry the bride would bring with her, as well as the settlement if the marriage ended in divorce. Often the inheritance rights of any children of the marriage were included. Agreements even allowed the wife's dowry to return to her father's estate, should she die without children.[1]

When Elizabeth I of England contemplated marriage, her agents tried to hammer out an agreement with the agents for the Duke of Alençon, a Frenchman, twenty years her junior but, nevertheless, a potential mate. In June of 1579, Alençon's agents crossed the Channel to work out the contract. They demanded Alençon be crowned King immediately after the wedding, a large pension be paid to him throughout his life, and that he have the right to remain a practising Catholic. The Queen's agents asked Alençon to forswear any contribution towards expenses should France go to war against the Netherlands. Queen Bess needed more than a lawyer; the entire Privy Council had to agree to the terms. They didn't and the marriage never took place.[2]

In America, premarital agreements used to be considered the domain of the very rich, who used them mainly to limit the amount of money a husband or wife could inherit. Prior to the 1970s the courts would not uphold an agreement that spelled out conditions in the event of a divorce. Women were not allowed to waive their rights to maintenance (it would have been unthinkable for men to receive maintenance). Remember, property usually went to the owner, most often the husband, so maintenance was the only point of negotiation in a divorce settlement. This was a way of protecting the little woman and preventing her from becoming a public charge.

And women have often shown a romantic reluctance to sign such agreements. The actor Kim Basinger is reported to have quipped, 'If you can't be sure of your man then there's no point in going into marriage in the first place.'[3]

Courts also worried that antenuptial contracts that waived maintenance also promoted divorce, because the husband would have no obligations if he left. But now that it's okay for women to work and for women to be considered equal, support is no longer a major concern of the law.

Premarital agreements crop up everywhere these days, including the corporate world. When James Stewart, one-time chairman of Lone Star Industries, Inc. in the United States, married one of his five wives, he billed the company US$16,795 in legal fees for his prenuptial agreement and was reimbursed.[4]

When Charles Lazarus, who made a fortune as chief executive of the American company Toys Я. Us, was sued for violating an obscure stock exchange trading rule, he pleaded not guilty. His explanation: the stock that had been traded was owned by his wife, sex therapist Helen Kaplan, and they had a prenuptial agreement that kept her money separate from his. He won his case.

PRENUPTIAL AGREEMENTS
in the UNITED STATES

In the United States, where prenuptial agreements have long been part of the marriage scene, the agreements supersede state laws. Most state courts will uphold prenuptial agreements, providing they do not leave one spouse destitute (the public policy issue). Nor do some state laws permit agreements that are thought to facilitate divorce. The courts would not uphold an agreement that required partners to divorce in five years. A judge in the State of Utah recently overturned an agreement because it was 'against public policy to facilitate the break-up of a marital relationship'.[5]

Agreements must be 'fair and reasonable' when made and not 'unconscionable' at the time they are carried out. Needless to say, the terms are difficult to define. A Texas judge ruled in 1990 that, 'In determining whether a contract is unconscionable or not, the court must look to the entire atmosphere in which the agreement was made, the alternatives if any, which were available to the parties at the time of the making of the contract; the non-bargaining ability of one party, whether the contract is illegal or against public policy and whether the contract is oppressive or unreasonable.'[6]

The law does not protect people from signing bad agreements. As one judge put it, 'A party who knowingly has entered into a lawful contract which may be improvident is not entitled to protection from the court(s) which are not free to change his contract for him or to avoid the results thereof.'[7] The fact that an agreement may not seem fair doesn't help either, if you signed.

An agreement that violates a child's right to support will also not stand up to court scrutiny. Some American states reserve the right to declare an agreement unenforceable if circumstances change drastically.

Courts will also take a look at the way the agreement was executed. Laws may vary slightly, but under the general law of contracts, there are four basic reasons an agreement can be invalidated:

1 Fraud.

2 Failure to fully disclose assets.

3 No separate representation.

4 The agreement was signed under physical duress.

A court in the United States declared unenforceable an agreement signed when 'the husband sprang [it] upon the wife the day before a well planned elaborate wedding was to occur in a large suite at the O'Hare International Airport in Chicago'. He pulled the agreement from his pocket when the parties were at the jewellers picking up their wedding rings. Passage had already been booked for a honeymoon cruise to Europe, the wife's trousseau had been purchased, invitations for the large wedding had been sent. The husband had made no mention of the agreement prior to the surprise at the jewellery store. The wife certainly did not have independent counsel of her own choosing. 'The only evidence of legal advice is that within twenty-four hours before the wedding, when the husband first presented the antenuptial agreement and she rebelled, she spoke on the telephone to his lawyers'.[8]

As for signing your own handwritten agreement, this could be a problem. Film director/producer Steven Spielberg wrote one on a piece of paper, without consulting a lawyer. Then he and his wife to be, Amy Irving, signed it. The agreement didn't hold up in court and Irving received one of the largest divorce settlements in Hollywood, reputed to be close to US$100 million.[9]

CURRENT SITUATION in AUSTRALIA

Prenuptial agreements have not been recognised in Australia, but the federal government has recently announced amendments to the *Family Law Act* that include the recognition of such agreements. And they make sense. The advent of equitable distribution laws, a rise in the divorce rate, a high number of second marriages and an increase in the number of working women with their own assets have done away with the old, romantic notions of sharing for many couples. It is not surprising that they might want to use the prenuptial agreement as a marriage contract, spelling out the consequences of a break-up or death in much the way partners in a business would sign a contract. You might look at a prenuptial agreement as the economic contract of a marriage. But beware: all too often they can be agreements made between unequals.

Responses to prenuptial agreements in Australia have been mixed. Some lawyers, such as Owen Trembath, a high-profile Sydney lawyer, feel that they can set up a sort of 'reverse psychology'. While they may deal with the practicalities of separation, divorce and the split-up of property, they also set the scene for a break-up.

Even though prenuptial agreements have not been legally recognised, they have been considered as evidence in cases where couples have split after a relatively short time and where their financial situations have not been changed much by the marriage. Decisions of the Family Court have recognised that over a long period of time, the property of partners to a marriage merges. Where agreements do not reflect this and could be seen as unfair, the courts will override the agreement. Family Court judge Joe Goldstein points out that as soon as there are children in a relationship, the courts look beyond any personal agreement made between partners.[10]

Other lawyers are more optimistic about their value. In a society where 35 per cent of first marriages and 40 per cent of second marriages break up, it can be perfectly sensible, if unromantic, to plan ahead. It can save considerable heartache at the time of the break-up—providing, of course, that both partners had good advice when they agreed to the contract in the first place. There are stories of starry-eyed women, swept off their feet by future husbands, who will sign anything. And there are stories of women from wealthy families whose families insist that a break-up does not mean that the family fortune gets split fifty–fifty.

DRAWING UP A PRENUPTIAL AGREEMENT

It can cost anything from $400 to $1500 to have an agreement drawn up. Partners should have separate legal advice, both to protect their separate interests and to ensure that they understand what they are signing. Part of the agreement should be that it is regularly updated to reflect changes in circumstances.

Perhaps the main advantage of prenuptial agreements is that they make explicit the financial interests and expectations of both partners. It seems that without such agreements, most couples enter marriage with very vague notions about each other's financial assets, likes and dislikes. This undoubtedly makes for traumatic revelations if and when financial settlements have to be made after couples have lost that loving feeling. For example, the American actor Tatum O'Neal has allegedly decided that the US$6 million in her prenuptial agreement is insufficient, and she is now fighting for US$55 million of tennis supremo John McEnroe's estimated US$150 million fortune.[11]

If you are getting married and your husband-to-be wants

you to sign such an agreement, there are a few things you should know. Under the *Family Law Act*, you are entitled to certain benefits from your marriage, whether it ends in death or divorce. When you sign an agreement, you may be giving up some of these benefits that are otherwise yours by right. Depending on what sort of agreement you sign:

1. You may be giving up your right to inherit property under your partner's will or under the intestate laws of your state.

2. You may be giving up your right to an equitable distribution should your marriage end in divorce.

3. You may be giving up other rights, such as the right to maintenance.

WHY YOU MIGHT WANT a PRENUPTIAL AGREEMENT

While the primary purpose of such agreements is still to protect the money of the wealthier spouse, agreements have also become almost mandatory in the United States for second marriages where husband and wife want to keep their finances separate so that their children from a first marriage can inherit their property.

Couples who have been through terrible divorces the first time around want to be sure that things will be easier should the second marriage not work out.

Prenuptial agreements are also the place for some couples to hammer out potential child custody, child support and visitation rights. They also use the prenuptial contract as a place to discuss other details of the marriage, even going so far as to specify the number of times each week they will have sex. One can imagine a tired old couple in their bedroom, valiantly trying to live up to the obligations of their agreement. The courts are less interested in these personal details and are less likely to care about enforcing them. Premarital agreements serve as a plan for the dissolution of the marriage, not for the conduct of the marriage.

SOME REASONS WHY A WOMAN MIGHT WANT A PRENUPTIAL AGREEMENT

---

1. She has a lot more money than the man she is planning to marry and wants to keep control of her own money.

2. She is marrying for the second time and wants to protect whatever money she has.

3. She does not know how the courts might divide her assets should the marriage end in divorce, so she wants to establish her own terms.

4. She thinks it will eliminate problems should the marriage end in divorce.

5. She has children from a previous marriage and wants to be sure the children are protected.

6. She has a family business and doesn't want it to end up with his family.

7. She is a partner in a business and her partners want to be sure that control of the business will not pass outside the firm.

8. She is the daughter of wealthy parents or grandparents who insist she have such an agreement.

Prenuptial agreements hit deep psychological nerves. Most lawyers can tell you of agreements that were never signed. One tells of a couple who fought so bitterly that they stormed out of his office, never married *and* never paid him.

Prenuptials can imply a lack of trust, a signal that the one who wants the agreement will also want to control the marriage. If you are marrying a man whose sees his money as his source of power, he may want you to sign the agreement so that he will not lose this power.

Women who have money may want agreements just to be

sure they are not being married because they are rich. The willingness of the groom-to-be to sign an agreement at least gives some indication that his commitment is not only to her money. A woman who saw her own parents fight bitterly over money when they divorced may want an agreement in order to avoid the kind of acrimony she witnessed.

Premarital agreements are signed before the wedding, at a time when couples are supposed to be most in love. For first marriages, especially, it's hard to think about the marriage ending. So, why do people sign them? A friend, who signed a disastrous agreement, says, 'I didn't want to show that I wanted anything. I thought it was a matter of principle.' She signed an agreement in which she gave up all rights to income and marital property, despite her lawyer's advice not to sign.

Another woman revealed that eight years after she signed an agreement, she was still incensed about it. But like many women, she didn't want to face the embarrassment of calling off the marriage.

Although the idea is repugnant to many women, I suspect that few will react as did the fictional Pauline McAdoo in a recent novel by Dominick Dunne, An Inconvenient Woman. The beautiful, impeccably bred Pauline has been asked to sign an agreement by her soon to be husband's lawyer. Instead of signing, Pauline flings an inkwell at the lawyer and storms off to Paris. Frightened of losing her, the groom-to-be fires the lawyer, rushes off to Paris and presents her with a fabulous diamond engagement ring. And, just to make sure, immediately after the wedding, presents her with an incredible Van Gogh painting.

Should you sign an agreement and then want to break it, you will have a hard time. Tim Peters, former husband of Sallie Bingham, the American media heiress, signed an agreement agreeing to waive all claims to alimony. When the couple divorced in 1990, Mr Peters went to court in the state of

Kentucky to try and change the terms. The judge said that Mr Peters 'may now feel he made a bad bargain', but this wasn't sufficient grounds for revoking the agreement. In fact, the judge added that he thought Mr Peters had married Ms Bingham 'for her money and stayed married to her because of the material benefits that the relationship conferred'.[12]

On the other hand, the late Jacqueline Onassis reportedly reopened negotiations with lawyers after the death of her second husband Aristotle Onassis, and received more money than the original contract mandated.

To challenge a prenuptial agreement, as with any contract, you must prove that the agreement is not valid. For example, if you want to break an agreement because you say you were forced to sign it, you must be able to prove this to the court.

A judge in the United States overturned a prenuptial agreement which provided that each party's earnings during the marriage would remain separate property. One attorney drafted the agreement and testified that he advised both parties. During the marriage, all expenses were paid from the earnings of one spouse, while the other spouse invested all earnings. The court ruled that not only is full and fair disclosure necessary, but each party must be advised by an independent lawyer.[13]

If your husband-to-be says, 'Oh, just sign it now, I'll change it later', run for the hills. He may leave you more in his will, but men seldom change their agreements.

Only you can decide whether you are willing to sign a prenuptial agreement, but should you be asked to do so, there are a few rules of the game that you would be wise to understand. Of course, you can always say no.

WHAT TO CONSIDER BEFORE SIGNING

1   Be sure you have your own lawyer, even if you husband-to-be is paying for it. (Of course, if you don't have proper counsel, the agreement could be voided at a later date, which may be exactly what you want. In which case, you already know the game and probably don't need this chapter.)

2   While agreements may be valid without them, be sure your lawyer asks for as much financial disclosure as possible. If you are worried that there might not be any assets, remember that even billionaires like Donald Trump can have financial problems. You might ask for some money to be put in trust or into a non-cancellable insurance policy if future payments are involved and you think your ex might not make good on his agreement.

3   Inflation is always a problem, so perhaps your lawyer could suggest an inflation clause that increases the amount of money you receive by the annual rate of inflation.

4   It's also a good idea to try and set conditions under which the agreement might be renegotiated—perhaps after a certain number of years or the birth of a child. One woman who asked her husband to sign an agreement gave him 10 per cent of her assets each year, until he had 50 per cent. Remember, if you want to change or revoke the terms of the contract, do it in writing.

5   Sometimes you might ask for money up front. However, the transfer should be made after the wedding. If you get the money before you are married, there may be a tax involved. Once you are married, there is no tax on any money transferred between a husband and wife.

6   If you and your husband are partners in business, you might include a buy-out agreement and a valuation agreement in order to avoid a messy battle in the event of a divorce.

Asking for an agreement can be hard. You have to bring up the realities of money at a time when you are only supposed to be thinking about love. However, this might also be a good time to talk about your finances in general, and how you plan to manage your money.

The late Roy Cohn, who drafted one of the three agreements signed by Donald and Ivana Trump, suggested that his clients, usually wealthy men, resort to a series of white lies. Cohn proposed that Mister X go to his fiancée with the idea of a prenuptial agreement. If she says, 'Oh, I'm shocked', Mister X can say, 'I trust you completely, but my family won't allow it.' Other lawyers suggest that the person wanting the agreement should pretend it is the lawyer's idea.

While this is a somewhat cute approach, which may have worked for some rich older men marrying attractive younger wives (it is seldom that you see a rich young woman marrying a poor old man), it is probably not an approach that bodes well for the success of the marriage. If you want an agreement because you want to be sure you will continue to have control over your own finances, it is better to say so directly.

One wealthy bride-to-be asked her future husband to sign an agreement. He objected. In order to avoid a fight, she placed all of her assets in a trust, so as to keep them separate when she married. Other brides may decide to take the risks that marriage entails rather than pursue the idea of an agreement.

When both husband and wife are partners in professional practices they might want to decide ahead of time that their practices will remain separate and that the only marital assets they will divide on divorce will be personal property, their home and any investments they have jointly made.

Couples who might not have considered a premarital agreement are sometimes asked to do so by what lawyers call 'interested third parties'. When there is family money, a parent or grandparent may put pressure on a daughter or grandson to obtain an agreement—sometimes even threatening to cut off the potential heir who does not want to ask his or her future partner to sign. In the United States, partners in law firms and owners of businesses now often insist that all the partners have agreements to ensure that a spouse who is not a partner in the business will not be entitled to a chunk of the business as part of a divorce settlement.

Some lawyers advise clients who are signing prenuptial agreements to build in payout schedules that take into account tax laws. For example, if you and your husband own a house together and you will end up with the house, the agreement should include the possible tax on the house, should you decide to sell it.

One of the biggest problems with prenuptial agreements is the possibility that circumstances may change. You might sign an agreement that will not be enforced until twenty years later. Predicting your financial conditions that far ahead can be exceedingly difficult. As more and more agreements are being signed, more and more case law is evolving that suggests that courts may eventually look at an agreement to see, not if it was fair when it was signed, but if it is fair when it is enforced. An American decision in the 1980s addressed this issue. A couple signed an agreement that was fair and reasonable at the time of the signing. After a fourteen-year marriage, the husband's assets had grown to US$8 million. His annual income was US$250,000. The couple's standard of living had changed dramatically during the course of the marriage. The US$200 a month alimony the wife had agreed to receive for ten years if the marriage ended was now 'unconscionable' because circumstances had changed. The judge held that this was enough for him to set aside the agreement.[14]

Changed circumstances can mean that the equality of earnings you had counted on might not materialise, but in signing a prenuptial agreement you might have signed away your right to maintenance. Women who do this should be extremely careful. Despite the gains women have made, men still continue to earn more, even when they are in the same profession. If you don't consider and admit that your income might not keep pace, you could find yourself signing a 'mine is mine, yours is yours' agreement that will prove disastrous should something happen to your marriage.

There is little hard evidence that men and women behave differently when it comes to signing prenuptial agreements. Men who are asked to sign such agreements by their future wives do not seem any happier about signing than do women. But many lawyers have anecdotal evidence that women, especially women who earn their own money, are making mistakes that men are less likely to make when it comes to prenuptial agreements.

MISTAKES WOMEN MAKE

1 They want to keep everything for themselves

One woman who was marrying for the second time had inherited several million dollars from her first husband. She didn't want any of it to go to husband number two. She wanted it all to go to her children, and insisted on setting this down in an agreement. After the marriage, her now husband took over a small company that he has built into a business worth several hundred million dollars. They live in great style. To all their friends it is a great marriage. But underneath it all, she is seething. Why? It seems she went to her now wealthy husband and asked him to give her a few million dollars so that she would have a little more to give to her children. He turned her down. She continues to live a glamorous life, too accustomed to the comforts of their marriage to leave, too long away from her own career to turn it into a big money maker, but too angry with her husband to really enjoy his riches. 'Women,' says one matrimonial lawyer, 'tend to be so concerned about the money they earned, that they try to protect it at the expense of a long-term gain.'

2 They won't take any risks

When a friend married a few years ago, she now reluctantly admits she signed an agreement with her husband to buy a large house in the country. The house was to be owned jointly, and each would contribute a certain amount of capital and expenses. You can probably guess the rest. They bought the house at an absolute low in the real estate market. They agreed that if they ever split, he would buy her out. This was just before a major real estate boom. When the split came, the house was worth over a million dollars and she had to be satisfied with her original low investment.

3 They were given bad advice

My friend Margaret was marrying for the second time. The man, who was from another state, seem ideal. He was a partner in a law firm and seemed to be very prosperous. Her lawyers advised her not to have a prenuptial agreement. They believed the man had more assets than my friend did and that an agreement would be detrimental to her should the marriage break up. Her lawyers were wrong. When the marriage broke up, it turned out he was broke. In fact, he ended up suing her for some of the money and a lot of the marital property, including the bed-sheets that she had paid for.

POSTNUPTIAL
AGREEMENTS

If you are already married and don't have an agreement, there is always the 'postnup'. This works like the prenuptial agreement, but might be more difficult to introduce into the marriage.

There are a variety of reasons for wanting a postnuptial agreement. A lawyer reports preparing an agreement for a long married couple. The wife thought the husband was taking a risky business decision and she wanted an agreement that would safeguard a certain amount of assets.

You might inherit a great deal of money and want to be sure that it won't become marital property, or you and your partner might decide to start a business. A postnuptial agreement could settle ahead of time what would happen in the event of either death or divorce.

Or you might just be worried about the marriage.

In the end, no agreement will ensure a good marriage, and no agreement will mean that you won't have a messy fight, should you divorce. If an agreement is made between unequals, this could lead to resentment and anger that might affect an otherwise good marriage. If you want an agreement because you think the marriage will not work out, maybe you should think again before marrying.

FIVE

COMING apart

AT THE TIME OF THEIR divorce, Americans Gerarda Wilhelmina Schoos Unkel Pommerenke and her husband Roger owned a home worth US$125,000. When Ms Pommerenke was awarded only US$7,500 as a divorce settlement, she appealed the decision—and lost. Ms Pommerenke's practice of sunbathing 'topless' in the presence of a male guest who 'felt free to be in his "underwear" or nude in the presence of his host's wife and in the absence of his host' did not influence the judge. Nor did it matter that Ms Pommerenke was guilty of adultery. What mattered was the US$95,582 that Roger Pommerenke saved before their marriage and used for the down payment on their home. Mr Pommerenke kept his separate property. The marital property was divided equally.

The judge decided the case according to modern divorce law. No more judgments about the good wife or the bad husband.

In an Australian case that set a similar scene for behaviour and fault, the Full Court of the Family Court decided that the conduct of parties during the marriage was relevant only if it had financial consequences.[1] It was alleged that the wife had nagged the husband for years, had threatened and attacked him, taken complete charge of his salary and wouldn't let him use the family car. When she applied for maintenance after the divorce, the magistrate who heard the case determined that the wife's behaviour was so bad that it would be unjust to award her maintenance. This decision was overturned, with the court affirming that maintenance was based on need and capacity to pay.

In another case where 'financial consequences' of behaviour did affect a decision of the court, significant maintenance was awarded to a wife whose husband had assaulted her, causing deafness in one ear.[2] In this case the wife's health problems and reduced earning capacity were taken into account in awarding her maintenance.

Welcome to the divorce revolution: a reversal of old rules that has changed the look of divorce in four ways:

◆ *The grounds for divorce have changed.*
◆ *Property settlements have changed.*
◆ *Spouse maintenance has changed.*
◆ *Child support and child custody have changed.*

GROUNDS for DIVORCE

Twenty years ago, the kind of behaviour exhibited by Ms Pommerenke would have been worthy of lurid headlines in the local paper. Adultery was only one reason for granting a divorce. Others were desertion, separation for five years, cruelty, imprisonment and insanity. If the wife was caught playing around, she was usually left with nothing. If the husband was the guilty party, he usually paid dearly for his errant ways.

Moral judgments are increasingly removed from the financial decisions of divorce. In the 1960s, as a student, I lived for a short time with my grandmother and her sister. Products of a very different social context, they guiltily hid their evening sherry if anyone came to the house. And the fact that 'Aunty' was a divorcee was never mentioned. Both my great-aunt and my grandmother believed it was shameful that her husband had deserted her, and my rather different values could not erase the stigma they both felt.

HISTORY of DIVORCE

The word 'divorce' comes from the Latin *divortium*, which allowed for the dissolution of a marriage by mutual consent. The ancient Romans had pretty well figured out the economics of divorce. If there was a divorce and no adulterous activity, the wife could recover her dowry within one year. If the wife was guilty of adultery, the husband got to keep one-sixth of the dowry. If the wife had done something less damaging, the husband kept only one-eighth of the dowry. If the husband was fooling around, he had to return the dowry immediately. He could hang on to the dowry for six months if he had committed a less serious offence. If, said Roman law, both parties had been guilty of adultery, the law acted as if neither party was guilty— that is, the wife got her dowry back after one year.

THE ENGLISH EXPERIENCE

Before 1867, divorce in England was a matter for the ecclesiastical or church courts. In effect, they did not permit divorce but under extreme circumstances allowed for a form of judicial separation. Those extreme circumstances had to involve far more than cruelty. In a case of cruelty considered in 1790, the results were a refusal to allow judicial separation on the public policy grounds that the general happiness of married life should be upheld—and not be undermined by a few individuals. In this case it was stated, 'The happiness of some individuals must be sacrificed to the greater and more general good.'[3]

In 1857 it became possible for a wife to cease 'cohabiting' with her husband and to obtain maintenance from him, but neither party could remarry. The only way to get what we would today call a proper divorce was through an Act of Parliament. This was a costly and lengthy procedure and involved consideration by the House of Lords, which would investigate the situation in great detail—not a prospect that any individual could have fancied. In fact, the procedure was confined to the very wealthy. Between 1715 and 1852, only 244 divorces were obtained in England, at a cost of between £700 and £1000 each. And not surprisingly, of the 244 cases only four were granted to women, who presumably had neither the money nor the stomach to go through what was a very public and humiliating experience.

Women at this stage—and until well into the 20th century in both England and Australia—also suffered the indignity of having to establish more grounds than did their husbands if they wished to initiate a divorce. A man could divorce his wife for adultery alone. But a wife had also to prove aggravating circumstances, such as bigamy, incest, cruelty or desertion. The distinction was based on the very strongly held belief that the consequences of a wife's adultery were far more serious than those of a man. She could, through her sexual liaisons, bear a child that was not the husband's—and he wouldn't know. He, on the other hand, could spread his seed elsewhere without it damaging the disposition of estates and titles—at least not his own. There were no public policy concerns here about the perpetuation of the general happiness of marriage.

Behind this, of course, was the fact that the laws were made for and about people of social class and distinction. In the upper echelons, a woman's primary role was to provide a male heir to continue her husband's family line. It was not until the emergence of a middle class and the decline, during the Industrial Revolution, in the value of estates and titles as a source of wealth that the need for more available divorce was seen by Parliament and the courts as justifiable. By 1857, when the *Divorce Act* was passed, the ecclesiastical courts lost their say in matters of divorce and judicial separation. These became the province of a new Court for Divorce and Matrimonial Causes.

THE AUSTRALIAN EXPERIENCE

In Australia, we moved through similar stages in the development of divorce law until the enactment of the *Family Law Act* in 1975, which introduced the no-fault divorce. From 1975, under the new Act, 'irretrievable breakdown of the marriage' became the only ground for divorce. This was conclusively presumed to exist after the parties had lived separately for at least twelve months.

No-fault divorce eliminated the need for blame. When adultery was the principal grounds for divorce, the husband often staged an 'assignation', in order to provide the necessary reason for the courts to dissolve a marriage. George Bernard Shaw, in his 1908 play *Getting Married*, depicts a scene in which a couple feign an argument that ends with the husband striking the wife, in the presence of a witness, so that the wife could obtain a divorce on the grounds of physical cruelty.

Divorce reformers who supported no-fault believed it would eliminate the need for 'corroborated perjury'.[4] No-fault was meant to be a truth in divorce law. Couples could now obtain a divorce, by mutual consent, without trumped-up grounds.

But the new divorce laws brought other problems. One that has been discussed at length is the change to the notion of fault and punishment. This change in social values created enormous problems in the early stages of the new law, where the partner who genuinely felt that they had contributed no fault to the marriage breakdown could still find him or herself divorced—with no recriminations and no one officially to blame. A friend of my mother's, now divorced for almost twenty years, is still bitter about the fact that her husband had numerous affairs, left her for a younger woman, deceived her about his relationships and his assets, and walked away scot-free. She, who had not worked for twenty years, received maintenance for a year in order to 'retrain' and join the work force. She feels she did all the right things and was punished anyway.

Another change in family law is the assumption that women can take care of themselves—financially and emotionally. Some can. But when early decisions under the *Family Law Act* were made, many previously married women were incapable of adapting easily to an independent lifestyle.

Even so, it has been typical under the new divorce laws in Australia for more women than men to apply for divorce. In spite of the very identifiable trend of women moving rapidly down the economic scale after divorce, while their ex-husbands tend to move up, women take the risk of divorcing. They report that peace of mind—and escape from physical and emotional violence—is worth the financial insecurity that results from the sacrifice of the breadwinner's contributions.

A divorce is a declaration from the Family Court that legally ends a marriage. It is known as a *decree absolute of dissolution of marriage*. This is granted a calendar month after the initial granting of a *decree nisi*, which is given when the court decides that a marriage has broken down. The *decree absolute* is sent to the divorcing parties about six to eight weeks after the court proceedings.

To obtain a divorce in Australia, where one federal law covers all the states, you have to convince the court that your marriage has ended and that there is no chance of your resuming a marriage relationship. You must also show that you and your husband have lived apart—that is, have been separated—for at least twelve months.

The court needs to be convinced of the separation, and may look for signs of any or all of the following:

◆ *A sexual relationship.*
◆ *Living in the same house.*
◆ *Looking after money together.*
◆ *Going out together socially.*
◆ *Contact during periods of separation.*
◆ *Raising of the children of the marriage.*
◆ *Whether friends and family know you have separated.*

You and your husband can be separated and still live in the same house, but you need to be able to prove that· you no longer share your lives or have a sexual relationship, that you no longer cook, shop and clean for each other, or operate in the world together as a couple. The court may want corroborative evidence of this from friends, neighbours or relatives. They may be required to put their evidence in an affidavit to be given to the court with your application for divorce.

In other words, anyone can get a divorce. If you want the divorce, and more and more women do, you can leave the marriage just as easily as your husband. By the same token, if he wants to leave and you don't want him to, this in itself is considered as evidence of 'irreconcilable differences' and, providing the separation is proven, the divorce will take place.

Some couples, for religious or other reasons, do not want to live together but do not want a divorce. They can agree instead to a legal separation. This is a formal document that sets out their rights and obligations, such as the support and child custody arrangements the couple have with each other. If you have a legal separation, you cannot remarry.

PROPERTY
and DIVORCE

Far more sweeping than the change towards easier divorce is the change in the economics of divorce. Underlying the decisions of the court in relation to dividing up the property is the idea of the husband and wife as economic partners, regardless of which partner earned the money.

Gender-based rules, written to protect the wife, have gone. The change in the law matched a change in society, although many women think that the change in the law came first. Where the old laws protected the traditional wife, even older women are now regarded as capable of working and supporting themselves. Women are no longer seen as dependent and in need of maintenance from ex-husbands for the rest of their lives.

The laws also protect the state. Like husbands who resent having to support wives and children who have left them, the state has found it less than desirable to support the wives who were left by 'other' men. The law increasingly puts the onus on divorcing partners to support themselves and their children. The state does not wish to become the equivalent of the husband and father, paying for women and children through Social Security.

PROPERTY DIVISION

When it comes to divorce, there are several kinds of property: yours, his and ours. Lawyers refer to *marital* (ours) and *separate* (yours or his) property. Under Australian family law, married couples may own property jointly or as individuals. There is no assumption that certain assets (such as the matrimonial home) must be owned equally, or that spouses have any entitlements to various assets because of their marriage.

If a dispute arises over who is entitled to what, the court has broad discretion over how it distributes the property. All property may be divided, regardless of how it was obtained, how it was used during the marriage or in whose name it is registered. Even property owned before the marriage, or inherited or given to one spouse, may be part of the assets that are divided on divorce.

Once all the property has been identified and valued, the court considers contribution—the financial and non-financial input, both direct and indirect, in acquiring, maintaining and improving the property. It includes the spouses' contributions to the welfare of the family, including that of homemaker and parent, although as Jocelynne Scutt, feminist lawyer and writer, points out, beware the court that carries with it the vestiges of the old world. Scutt shows that there is a fine tradition in the law of continuing to undervalue women's non-financial contribution, even when they have freed a husband to work at financial contributions. It is not surprising, she says, in a society where 'money' equates with 'importance', that the unpaid work that women do is sometimes not even regarded as 'work'.[5]

Property settlements can be made either by order of the court or by consent orders. When settling the property, the courts will look at:

◆ *what the parties have contributed to acquiring and maintaining assets in the past.*
◆ *each party's ability to support themselves financially at present and in the future.*

The court will look at all the assets acquired during the marriage or purchased with money from the marriage, such as a house, car and savings. A wife's contribution as homemaker and parent is included. Usually there is a loading, such as 60:40

or 55:45, in favour of the parent who has the children.

Even so, the reality is that women after divorce head very quickly for a lower standard of living than they previously enjoyed. Their chances statistically of being able to earn as much as their partners are slim. Men, on the other hand, rarely take responsibility for the children—and the time, effort and cost that they involve. They frequently move on to make more money than before the divorce—and have fewer financial responsibilities. As Keith Wearne, an accountant and adviser on property settlements, states, 'Even when women receive a greater share of the assets on divorce, men's greater earning power and freedom to move about often means that they benefit from no longer having the seemingly endless demands that kids and families make on the pocket.'[6]

'It does appear that the ripening fruit on the tree of marriage has all fallen into the husband's basket.'[7]

Eliminating marital fault from divorce did not eliminate fights between divorcing couples. With property at stake, divorcing couples began to battle over the value of property, ownership of property and even what constituted property. Property can start out as separate property; for example, your home may have been purchased with money that you had before marriage. But your husband, by making repairs or helping with the upkeep, may have gradually transformed it into property that the court sees as joint marital property.

In looking at the maintenance part of a property settlement, the court can consider more than just what you own in tangible form—the house, the car, savings accounts. It also considers the health of the parties, their earning capacity and their financial position in the future. If the husband has contributed to a superannuation policy (an option not available to the wife who has worked in the home or in part-time work), the court can take this into account and either increase the wife's share of the available assets or, if the superannuation is due in the foreseeable future, hold off the division until that time so that the wife can share the 'property'. They cannot, when the superannuation is still a long way from becoming due, regard it as actual property.

MAINTENANCE and DIVORCE

The *Family Law Act* makes provision for spouse maintenance, but orders for wife maintenance are rarely made. Lump-sum maintenance is also uncommon—in spite of the urban myths that abound and TV shows like *Absolutely Fabulous*. In reality, it seems there are few men these days who do not invest in legal advice to assist them in avoiding paying maintenance to ex-wives.

The *Family Law Act* states that a husband is liable to maintain a wife to the extent that he is reasonably able to do so, if and only if she is unable to support herself adequately.

The court takes into account the following in the awarding of maintenance:

◆ *The age and health of each of the parties.*
◆ *The income property and financial resources and the capacity for gainful employment.*
◆ *Whether either party has care and control of children aged under eighteen.*
◆ *Commitments (e.g. to maintain self or other family members such as aged parents, etc.).*
◆ *Pensions and superannuation entitlements.*
◆ *A reasonable standard of living.*
◆ *Whether maintenance would enable one party to improve their earning capacity by allowing them to undertake training, education, etc.*

◆ *The extent to which the maintained partner has contributed to the earning capacity, financial resources and property of the other party.*

◆ *The duration of the marriage and the extent to which this has affected the earning capacity of the person to be maintained.*

◆ *The need to protect the person who wishes to continue in a parenting role.*

◆ *Cohabitation with another person—the financial circumstances.*

◆ *Any other facts or circumstances that the court should take into account in the interests of justice.*

The court is not to take into account the entitlement of any party to Social Security in the form of an income-tested pension, allowance or benefit. This is designed both to take the burden off the state (and taxpayers) and to prevent the court from decreasing the amount of maintenance on the grounds that a pension is available.

As the divorce revolution has proceeded, intangible property has also come to be deemed divisible. Intangible property that is sometimes considered for division includes:

◆ *future earnings such as commissions on an insurance policy sold during the marriage.*

◆ *superannuation and other fringe benefits.*

◆ *stock options.*

◆ *professional goodwill.*

Professional degrees are another intangible property that increasingly are being defined as marital property, especially in the United States.

As an example, from America, of things to come, consider the story of Lorretta O'Brien. When she married in 1974, she was a teacher and her husband was starting medical school. He received his medical degree almost ten years later. Two months after that he filed for divorce. In a landmark decision, Ms O'Brien sued for an interest in that licence. The reasoning was simple. Even though the licence didn't appear to be marital property, it gave Dr O'Brien a passport to future earnings. Ms O'Brien, who had supported her husband during those early years, would have none of those future earnings unless the licence was deemed to be marital property. The New York Court of Appeals agreed with Ms O'Brien, and she was awarded 40 per cent of the value of the licence.

SUPERANNUATION

Possibly the largest asset for most couples, after the family home, is the husband's superannuation. While many women have superannuation, many do not. Or if they do, because they tend to leave jobs in order to have children, the value of the wife's superannuation is generally much less than her husband's.

In a study in 1988 entitled *Australian Women and Economic Security*,[8] the researchers found that only 35 per cent of women in paid employment had superannuation (representing only 15 per cent of women). In part, this was connected with women being more likely to have part-time, low paid and casual work. Frighteningly though, most women over age forty had not taken out superannuation as they believed their financial futures were secure because of their husband's superannuation scheme. A belief that they should also be rewarded for their efforts in freeing their partners to contribute to superannuation schemes would seem to be a reasonable proposition. But it is not one that the courts see quite so simply.

The Women's Electoral Lobby Family Law Action Group proposed in 1979 that the courts could and should be able to make a calculation as to the proportion (equal), in terms of years of contribution by homemaking and parenting, which the spouse who has not directly paid into the superannuation fund should receive. This could take the form of a court order for the contributing partner to assign the amount to the ex-spouse when the benefits fall due. Fifteen years later, their recommendations have still not been adopted.

The American case of Sandra Goldman is a good example of how superannuation can work against women. She was forty-six when, after a twenty-year marriage, she and her husband Peter, a neurosurgeon, divorced in 1987. The Goldmans have two children, Wendy and Gregory. Ms Goldman, a nurse, did not work during the marriage. Peter Goldman earned US$478,560 in 1986. From time to time he receives bonuses, and his corporate cheque account pays for various personal expenses. He has a large superannuation fund into which his corporation paid over US$200,000 during the three years prior to the divorce. In their divorce action, the judge awarded Ms Goldman US$1000 per week for eight years, part maintenance and part child support, and suggested that she brush up her nursing skills. Said the judge, 'Mrs Sandra Goldman's opportunity for future acquisition of capital assets and income certainly will never approach that of Dr Goldman. However, she has an opportunity to be gainfully employed and to invest wisely the distribution of assets pursuant to this judgement.' Oh yes, Ms Goldman was given the family home and its furniture, with the exception of her husband's guns and a gun cabinet, animal trophies, an elephant foot fireplace fender, shotgun shell loading equipment, gun cases and daughter Wendy's Raggedy Ann doll. She was also given a lump sum payment of US$216,000.

Ms Goldman's lawyers appealed the decision. The second judge agreed. Ms Goldman's award should have been based on the standard of living she had enjoyed during the marriage.

STANDARD of LIVING

Increasingly, the 'standard of living' is becoming an issue in Australian divorce cases. Keith Wearne, an accountant, explains that women and their advisers are now claiming that divorce should not leave one partner with every chance of improving his or her standard of living while the other faces an inevitable decline. Particularly after a long marriage between the partners, adjustments should be made to ensure that each maintains a similar standard of living. If this means that the one with greater earning potential and large superannuation entitlements pays out more over a longer period, then the law should support and facilitate this.

CELEBRITY GOOD WILL

Celebrity good will is another 'intangible' that has been included in the United States in the division of marital assets. It is a problem most of us won't have. In 1988 the actress and model Marisa Berenson and her husband, Richard Golub, divorced. Golub claimed that the increased value of Ms Berenson's career during the marriage was marital property and that he was entitled to some of the proceeds. The court agreed with Golub that Ms Berenson's celebrity status was indeed 'marital property', though he was not awarded any money.

THE NEW MAINTENANCE

There is no question that many women, and a few men, have benefited from the new property laws. But what happens when there is little property to divide? After property division, maintenance looms as a major divorce problem. The concept of maintenance has changed dramatically. Again eliminating any distinction between husband and wife, the new laws were enacted to eliminate the idea of the dependent wife getting a dole from her husband until either she remarried, he died, or she committed some act, such as living with another man, that would deprive her of her stipend.

With or without fault, maintenance is going the way of the

dinosaur. The trend, say many lawyers, is for women to be self-supporting. Instead of the long-term maintenance that used to be granted until a wife either died or remarried, maintenance except in long-term marriages (usually considered to be at least ten years), if it is awarded at all, is generally temporary.

The idea of spouse and child maintenance has changed dramatically over the past decades. Maintenance payments to a spouse are not automatic upon separation. An application must be made within twelve months of the divorce. If you don't have dependent children and you are able to work, the chances of your getting maintenance, regardless of what your ex-husband earns, are slim.

Maintenance payments are decided on the particular facts of the case, bearing in mind the need of one party to receive it and the ability of the other party to pay it.

Meredith and Michael, who had been married for twenty-two years, divorced. Michael, who was well paid and had generous superannuation benefits due within fifteen years, left and subsequently remarried. Meredith undertook a training course that would make her eligible for an adequate job within two years. Apart from the property settlement in which Meredith received half the value of the house and much of the furniture, the judge awarded her $1000 a month and a lump sum of $10,000 to help her find alternative accommodation. The judge made it clear that Michael, who had remarried and was planning a second family, would be able to reduce the monthly payment once Meredith had established herself in secure employment.

BANKRUPTCY

The payment of maintenance and the distribution of assets assumes that couples have accumulated some assets during their marriage. Frequently, that is not the case; instead, they may have piled up the debts. In such cases, divorce settlements become a question of dividing the debts. What happens to the jointly owned family home if one partner becomes bankrupt?

Normally, on bankruptcy the trustee has a right to take most of a bankrupt's real estate and personal property. This means that it is likely that a jointly owned matrimonial home will be sold. The non-bankrupt spouse will have first option to buy the bankrupt's share. If she (or occasionally he) can't afford it, a decision can be made to sell the home, with each partner receiving equal shares after the mortgage and expenses are paid. If the non-bankrupt spouse refuses to cooperate, the trustee can arrange a court order for the property to be sold, with equal shares going to the partners.

CHILD SUPPORT and CUSTODY

An even greater assumption about men and women's traditional roles was challenged with a series of new laws about child custody and child support. In the past, the father had the responsibility for supporting his children; the mother was considered responsible for taking care of them. So, when a marriage dissolved, the mother was awarded custody, and the father was ordered to pay child support and given visitation rights to his children. The new laws stressed equality. Both mother and father had to support the children. And, in an even greater break with tradition, fathers could have custody of their children, either joint physical custody or joint legal custody. What this meant was that the best interests of the child should be considered. In some cases, courts were able to decide that the best interests of the child were served when the mother had custody part of the time and the father the rest of the time, including arrangements that left parents driving their children back and forth to each other's houses on a weekly basis.

COLLECTION of MAINTENANCE

A big problem with maintenance can be collecting it. Although child maintenance is supposed to be paid until a child reaches eighteen, the reality is that payments have often tapered off before then and may have ceased altogether. At one stage it was estimated that up to 80 per cent of separated fathers in Australia were not paying child support. This meant that women were relying increasingly on Social Security, to the extent that the government took what many (mainly fathers) considered drastic action in the setting up of the Child Support Agency. The Agency manages the collection of maintenance money for children by either arranging for an employer to deduct payments or by having the parent send the money direct to the Agency.

Child support is assessed and collected by a Commonwealth agency as part of the Child Support Scheme. The courts have no power to make child support orders for children whose parents separated or gave birth to a child after October 1989. However, there are still many families whose child support may be determined or varied by the courts because they are ineligible for administrative assessment, or the maintenance is required urgently, or the children are over eighteen but still financially dependent.

In those cases, the *Family Law Act* spells out the duty to maintain the child as being a primary duty of parents—more important than all commitments other than those to support the parents themselves and any other person for whom there is a maintenance duty. Where child support orders are made according to the *Family Law Act* provisions, they can be registered with the Child Support Agency for enforcement. The money will be paid to the custodial parents by the Department of Social Security (DSS). Where possible, the order will be automatically withheld from the payer's salary and forwarded to the Agency by the employer.

The Agency, which is part of the Australian Tax Office, decides how much support should be paid. This is done by taking the income of both parents into account and making allowance for the costs of raising any natural or adopted children in their care. Where the parents cannot come to an agreement, the Agency applies a formula, set out by law, that determines the amount to be paid. It is designed to cover most cases and allows for a variety of family circumstances.

Sole parents are required by law to take action to obtain child support. They can either come to an agreement (that the DSS thinks is adequate) with the parent who is liable to pay, or they can apply for and have the Agency collect the payments. If you are in this position but fear violence from a former partner, you can arrange to be exempt from the scheme.

Where a parent who pays maintenance through the Child Support Agency is bankrupted, there is not the same priority given to the Agency as to the custodial parent who is owed maintenance. This means that other creditors receive their claims before the Child Support Agency, and that parents who have an agreement outside the Agency have higher priority with the trustee to collect their money.

BETTER off THAN YESTERYEAR?

Would a woman fare better under the old system, or is she better off today? The law assumes today that a woman can go out and work. So women are more likely to be awarded the new 'maintenance' rather than the old lifetime maintenance.

There are not a lot of figures available about the extent of maintenance currently being paid in Australia, but it is apparent that amounts paid are often inadequate and are often not paid in full. Women who remarry lose their spousal maintenance and are far less likely to receive child maintenance payments than women who have not remarried.[9]

Spouses who refuse to pay cannot be imprisoned for failing to pay. However, they can be imprisoned for contempt of court. One case that received wide publicity involved a man who quite happily agreed to serve a court sentence rather than pay any money to his ex-wife.

Were we better off before no fault and the idea of equitable distribution? Probably not. The idea that women were taken care of through maintenance, prior to the change in divorce laws, may be a myth. Critics of what some call divorce-on-demand cite as evidence statistics showing women plunged into poverty following the adoption of the no-fault divorce laws. But there is plenty of evidence that the old divorce days weren't so great either. Very few divorced women received maintenance under the old fault system. When they did, judges and ex-husbands used the doling out of maintenance as a way to control the wife's behaviour after a divorce. And, in those days, fault could be liberally defined. In one case, a divorce was granted to a husband whose wife's 'preoccupation with social and club activities and failure to prepare [her] husband's meals' constituted marital cruelty. If a woman was at fault, she didn't get any money at all.

Divorce laws have changed to accommodate the notion that women are capable of being independent—financially and emotionally. If you don't change with them, the law does not protect you. For the 36 per cent of Australian women who divorce, it is apparent that their ex-husbands are far more concerned with protecting their own interests than with being fair to their ex-wives. The way to provide protection—just in case you need it—is to assume a sense of responsibility and agency about your finances—and to know about his.

If you THOUGHT MARRIAGE was BAD. . .

IN THEORY, DIVORCE REFORM was supposed to liberate women and end the lying that previously surrounded divorce. Instead, many think that the new divorce laws have sent women into battle on foot while their husbands fire at them from armoured cars.

DIVORCE REFORM

First, let's look at what divorce reform under the 1975 Australian *Family Law Act* was meant to achieve. Guilt about divorce was to be eliminated, bitter fights were to end. Women would no longer be treated paternalistically, but would take their place as equals in the new economic partnership of marriage.

In 1975 the Women's Electoral Lobby anticipated the effects of the new divorce laws under the *Family Law Act*, stating:

. . . a woman will automatically be entitled to a fair share of the property and income she has helped her husband to acquire. A woman's full-time and unpaid career as enforced childminder and dinner producer at last has its rewards! [1]

Instead of the promised equities, it seems there have been increased inequities. Experts who promulgated the new laws are now taking a look at what they have brought about.

Articles have begun to appear in publications, from women's magazines to learned journals, about the unforeseen consequences of divorce reform. A report of a Parliamentary Inquiry into the *Family Law Act*, released in 1992, included 120 recommendations for improvement to the operation and interpretation of the Act.

Most women who have been through a divorce in the last twenty years don't need a sociologist or a report to tell them the new system is fraught with problems and that women have been the principal victims.

In 1991, 45,630 divorces were granted in Australia. An increasing proportion of those divorces are taking place within five years of marriage. Overall, about 37 per cent of marriages can be expected to end in divorce (closer to 40 per cent for second marriages). If you add the small number of marriage breakdowns that are never formalised by divorce, it can be safely estimated that 40 per cent of marriages will end in divorce within thirty years. Taking into account both widowhood and separation, only 53 per cent of today's couples can expect to be together after thirty years.

Anna Bryant's case is typical. Anna worked in paid work for ten years of her marriage and saw herself as financially and emotionally secure. Then she and her husband divorced. Anna would not agree to the settlement he proposed, which seemed to deny the value she placed on herself and her contributions to the marriage. Court proceedings in her divorce are still going on after three years. During that time she has had to move in with her parents (the home she and her husband owned was sold); she has sold her car and has had to borrow money from her parents.

Her lawyer believes there are several reasons Anna has had problems, and they are common to many women when marriages break down. One of her biggest problems was the lack of funds with which to pursue her case adequately. Legal aid is not generally available for contested divorces.

Anna didn't know about her husband's investments and had no idea of their value. He completely controlled the valuation of his assets. For example, he invested over $100,000 and then claimed it was worth only half. The court accepted his word. Frequently, with privately held stock, only the insiders really know the valuation. It is widely acknowledged in Family Court proceedings that men often hide their assets to prevent their wives from knowing how much money is in the family coffers. Some men have 30 or 40 different bank accounts in a variety of names. They apparently feel unabashed by this and feel it is legitimate, on the grounds that their wives would otherwise collect too much of 'their' money.

Instead of lying about fictional romances in order to obtain divorces, it seems that men have a tendency now to lie about the value of their assets and investments. Anna's plight revealed another aspect of the equitable distribution fall-out. She had not been in the paid work force for eight years when she separated, but was expected to retrain herself to go back to being a nurse. In her late forties, Anna does not relish the idea of heavy lifting and shift work. She is fighting for a better settlement so that she can start a business of her own and at least work her own hours.

WHO GETS WHAT?

In a study that looked at property decisions by the Australian Family Court over a six-year period, Jocelynne Scutt established that far from women taking the lion's share of property on divorce, they did not even get an equal share. While the court consistently sprouted the rhetoric of equal contributions and equitable settlement, it was patently obvious that the 'socialisation' of the judges and the lawyers presenting cases before the court affected the way decisions were made.

*. . . it should raise few eyebrows that monetary contributions are
viewed in a more substantial light than non-monetary contributions.
Not only are monetary contributions easily calculated and seen
(mortgage payments, water rates and land rates can be clutched at
securely by judges looking for landmarks) but our society is schooled in
the belief that 'money' means 'important'. Any work recompensed in
monetary terms is more important than work which is not: indeed, in
the world of economics, work which is unpaid is not classed as work.*[2]

The same is true in the United States, where:

*Judges devalue long-term homemakers' contributions to their families
and make unrealistic assumptions about older women's opportunities
in the paid work force. Thus dissolution awards give women small
shares of marital property and scant short-term alimony, leaving them
in extremis financially while their ex-husbands enjoy their former, or
even a more comfortable, standard of living.*[3]

In particular, the ideal of women now operating in the
world as independent people contrasts with the reality of
decisions of the Family Court. There is a definite tendency
when women have 'repartnered' between the break-up and the
settlement to regard them as 'needing' less. Women's prop erty
settlements on becoming independent from their first partner
assume that they can take their place in the world *without
needing any special protection*—but as soon as another man is on
the scene, the courts find these same women *less in need*! The
assumption is that as soon as they are connected to some other
man, they will give up their independence and become 'kept'
women.

Julie and Jon cohabited for three years, then married and lived
together for another four years. During that time Jon studied for
his PhD. Julie worked as a researcher, earning more with
overtime than he did as a junior academic. She also supported

him emotionally and as a 'wife'. She did all the shopping, cooking and nurturing—allowing him as much time as possible to work on his thesis. He then moved on to writing his first book. Again Julie did all the support work, as well as maintaining a full-time job. As a lecturer, Jon taught twelve hours a week and earned $40,000. With an interest-free loan of $85,000 from his mother, they bought a house for $126,000 in Sydney's Balmain—unpretentious but in a 'good' area. Julie and Jon agreed to pay half each of the mortgage, although Julie remembers paying all of the monthly repayments on many occasions (she didn't keep records). When Jon told her he was leaving, Julie consulted a solicitor who told her that after four years of marriage she could really only expect to receive half the value of the house—over and above the 70 per cent contribution that Jon's mother had provided. This meant that on a house now worth $280,000 in which she had lived and which she had maintained for four years, Julie was entitled to only $42,000—not even enough to put a deposit on a decent flat.

Whether women stay at home or participate in the paid work force, they can face some unpleasant situations when their relationships break-up.

Marion Drew, a middle-ranking public servant, thought her twenty-year marriage was secure until she noticed a Hayman Island entry on her husband's bankcard account. Neither she nor her husband had ever been to Hayman Island. Other strange things happened, but Marion ignored the signals. She couldn't believe anything was wrong with her marriage.

Her husband, an architect, managed everything. He even sold their house before Marion knew that the marriage was in trouble. The house was in his name, which she had agreed to ten years earlier because the holiday home they owned had been in her name. When the holiday home was sold to enable her husband to start his own business, they hadn't bothered to change the title on the family home. When they divorced, Marion was left with furniture she had before the marriage, a few thousand dollars and bitter memories. The money from the sale of both houses had all but disappeared. Her husband's architectural business, which had seemed to be flourishing before the Hayman Island incident, had somehow started operating at a loss so that she received none of the benefits from the money that had gone into it. Marion's ignorance cost her dearly.

EMOTIONAL FALL-OUT

The new laws have done little to reduce the acrimony of divorce. Part of the problem is that the laws are financial, but ending a marriage is emotional. Divorce fights centre around money, property and children, but the fights manifest the emotional problems of the marriage. Often they are about control and winning—probably paralleling the fights that took place during the marriage. Too often, they are still about punishment.

In a study carried out by the Institute of Family Studies,[4] comments from people interviewed make it clear that the *Family Law Act* has not eliminated bitterness and recriminations. Time and again, women complain about husbands hiding assets, and about their bullying tactics and emotional blackmail. They feel that when businesses are involved, husbands have the upper hand.

Interestingly, when women were actively involved in the running of a family business, separation and the division of property took place with fewer problems. Perhaps because the wife knew more about what the business was worth and because her contribution was visible, agreement about the settlement seemed easier.

> Betty decided at the age of sixty-eight that she wanted a divorce from her quite well established husband. She had not worked in the paid work force since her marriage forty years previously. She had, however, raised six children, and when they were all settled she decided she wanted a few years of peace before she died. In particular, she wanted to be able to phone her children without her husband complaining that it cost so much. She informed her husband that she wanted to separate for twelve months and then she wanted a divorce.

Within three weeks he had arranged an overseas trip with his oldest daughter and her husband. He gave the car, registered in his name, to his oldest grandson; he also gave each of his eight grandchildren $20,000 and spent over $100,000 on the overseas trip. By the time they ended up in court, Betty received $15,000, precisely half of the remaining assets. Her husband admitted that he was punishing her for humiliating him.

Nor does a change to an equitable law for division of property at divorce address the problem of control of assets during the marriage. Control continues to be in the hands of the husband or wife who earned the money.

Many of the assumptions of the *Family Law Act* were based on the ideal that women should no longer be treated as 'dependent', emotionally or financially. Overturning the paternalism of the English legal tradition, the Act presumed that women would be better off independent and self-sufficient. A fine sentiment. And appropriate, perhaps, for some well-paid working women. But it isn't so great for the woman who stays home to take care of the children and who gives up any career prospects of her own to help her husband.

Such women find that the ideal and the reality are still far removed, even in the 1990s. The courts do not give equal value to women's non-financial contributions, and while some allowance is usually made for their lesser earning capacity and for the fact that they look after four of every five children after divorce, many have literally found themselves on the streets looking for work.

The hardest hit is often the fifty-something woman who was in a long marriage. The problem, says one lawyer, is that today's fifty-year-old woman looks as the judge thinks forty should look. She looks like she can go out and work. So that's what the judge is telling her. Unless she is physically incapacitated in some way, she is now expected to retrain, re-educate and take her place in the world of paid work rather than be supported.

Women who stayed home and did not build their own careers have lost those years and are not compensated. The family home, which used to be awarded automatically to the wife, is now sometimes sold, and the proceeds are split. If there is an income-producing business, it frequently goes to the husband. The wife might be given a lump sum payment, but of course she does not have a business—nor the experience and resources—to generate income at the same level as her husband. 'His source of income and job satisfaction continues. She has to start again in the job market.'[5] Thus, even when the initial division is equal, over time the wife loses out.

BUSINESS ASSETS

There is no doubt that one of the new classes of the 'poor' in our society are women who have divorced and who are paying a high economic price for their lower earning capacity and the withdrawal of a partner's financial support.

This becomes clear in studies of what actually happens to business assets when marriages break up.[6] When wives had no ownership and played only minor roles in the running of the business, they expressed a high degree of dissatisfaction with the outcome of their cases. They emphasised their frustration at not being able to obtain fair valuations of the businesses or that the businesses had been deliberately manipulated in order to reduce their valuation between separation and distribution'.[7] In fact, they often state that they have felt pressured by the system, either by its costs or its personalities, to give up their questioning of information provided by their partners.

> Claire and her husband owned a farm on which they both worked on fencing, tractoring and general chores. She was one of the 80,000 women working on farms in Australia, constituting about 30 per cent of the farming work force.[8] During bad seasons, Claire travelled 100 kilometres a day to work as a secretary; she

also did typing at home. Without her income, they would undoubtedly have joined the ranks of the 39,000 farmers who left the land between 1986 and 1991.[9] Their children would not have been able to complete their education at boarding school, the fees for which were often paid by Claire.

When they split up and a divorce settlement was finally reached, not only did Claire start from the position that the farm was 'his', as he had inherited it from his parents, but she also found it difficult to articulate to her husband and his lawyer the contribution she had made. (Living as they did in a rural area, Claire's husband had been to school with the town's solicitor. She had to use a solicitor who lived 200 kilometres away.) They insisted that her contribution had been a paper one, primarily for tax purposes, and she found it almost impossible to get access to the financial documents needed to establish her interest in the property. The settlement eventually involved the husband keeping 75 per cent of the property, a decision he has still not accepted as fair. Part of the farm had to be sold to pay Claire. Of course, she had no chance of continuing on the land. She was also devastated that her husband and his lawyer used her sons— and their entitlement to inherit the property—as a form of blackmail. They put her in a position where, if she were to argue for her own share, she would be seen as depriving her children of what would be 'rightfully' theirs.

When men control the business and women have little idea of the finances, they can be sorely disadvantaged. When George and Helen split up, her lawyer wanted to include his computer consultancy service as a business asset to be shared between them. George simply said he would stop working if that were the case, so that there was no asset. By the time of the property settlement, the court decided there was no business to consider, even though George had been able—and would in future be able—to generate several thousand dollars a week.

BARGAINING
for the CHILDREN

And, for most women, the worst of all catastrophes now looms as a possibility. Equal rights language built into our laws suggests that a father has as much right to custody as a mother. Women's fear of losing their children has been added to the problems of divorce. While many men genuinely want custody of their children, lawyers across the country report that men will use this as a negotiating tool. They will threaten to seek custody of the children, then will agree to drop their demand for custody if you agree to take a smaller property settlement than you thought you deserved.

My solicitor was reluctant to ask for removal of any of the property from the matrimonial home as this could be disruptive for the children and could affect the custody dispute. As a result, I got nothing from the settlement except personal clothing.[10]

Women in these circumstances tend to think that once lawyers and the courts are involved, justice will prevail. Even if their husband is being unreasonable, they feel somehow that this will be recognised and sorted out. This is not always the case.

I was accepting his word for everything and I had no way of finding out what it was. He was lying. He kept threatening that he'd take the boys off me if I made too much fuss. In a way I expected the law to take over and what was right would happen, but that didn't come about at all. As I see it, it just amounts to who can afford the best barrister and who is the stronger of the two people, the bully one, who comes out on top.[11]

Matrimonial lawyers give several reasons women do not end up with the stake they should after a divorce:

1. Women do not have records of the family finances before the divorce. When a divorce looms, they discover that 'our' accountant has become 'his' accountant.

2. Women do not know the value of the family's assets.

3. Women do not have the money to hire the experts to locate and value the assets during a divorce.

4. Women do not have the money to support themselves during the divorce process if their husbands refuse to send money, so they settle for less than they should.

5. Women do not have the money to pay for lawyers.

6. When they do have money to pay, women still do not have the confidence and assertiveness to dictate the play in the divorce proceedings. Many are passive, assuming that the law and their lawyer will sort things out fairly and finally.

The reasons all add up to the same thing: a lack of financial equality at the bargaining table, and women having little sense of entitlement to assets accumulated during marriage.

DEALING with LAWYERS

For some women, a divorce is their first experience with lawyers and negotiations. They may be married to men who are routinely involved with contracts, negotiations and other details of business. For such women, the whole process of divorce can be more traumatic than for their husbands. Unfamiliarity with the process could also be a reason for settling for less.

Divorce is hell. No question. It's hell if you are Jane Smith or Jane Fonda with her looks, her fame and her money. Fonda, who was divorced from her second husband after a seventeen-year marriage, described the process as 'debilitating and frightening'.

The same women who were dominated financially during their marriages allow themselves to be dominated in the divorce. Some even hire lawyers who take on the role their husbands did, and let their lawyers make decisions for them. One woman, terrified of being alone, realised that she allowed her husband to talk her into giving up money by suggesting a reconciliation, which he never meant.

Should you be headed for a divorce, a compromising picture of your husband with another woman will not be nearly as important as a picture of his financial statement.

Most people who want a divorce begin making plans to bail out long before D-day. Men have been known to defer bonuses or even to postpone promotions until after a divorce, in order to lessen the amount of money they might have to pay their wives. Women who are contemplating a divorce are advised to stock up on groceries while their husbands are still paying the bills, and to stash away cash. And while strategies for bailing out of a marriage are usually financial, one woman found her husband's 'battle plan' in his briefcase. It called for him to begin body-building to improve his pectorals, in preparation for life with a younger woman.

If you already know about the family finances, you are way ahead of many women, especially those who are taken by surprise when their husbands want a divorce. Lawyers suggest that if divorce is at all a possibility, you should begin your preparations by seeking financial information. Of course, you are better off if you have been participating in the financial decisions of your marriage all along. You will need this information if you actually do get a divorce. If you don't get the divorce, having the information will still be helpful to you.

The hardest part of divorce, many women report, is making the decision that the marriage is over. How do you know when to even call a lawyer? There are several possible situations, each requiring some thought. If you think the marriage is in trouble but are not sure you want a divorce, you should do the following:

1. Visit a marriage counsellor. If you and your husband are able to discuss the problem, you can go together.

2. Begin gathering together all of the financial information you need, if you haven't already done so.

3. Consult a lawyer. Some people worry that consulting a lawyer is sure to lead you down the road to divorce. Others say that if you don't consult a lawyer, your husband may begin making secret divorce preparations and you will lose out.

If you think, as many women do, that your husband would never do anything underhanded, think again and pick up the phone. You don't have to commit yourself to a divorce. You can make perfectly clear the exploratory nature of your visit. The worst thing you can do is ignore the situation, thinking that your husband would never do anything to hurt you. He could. And you may find yourself doing things you never thought you could, such as looking through his pockets while he is in the shower, waiting until he is asleep to go through his wallet or rifling through the wastepaper basket. Unfortunately, while women know so little about their partner's money, this is not uncommon.

If your husband walks in one day, as happened to one woman shortly after she returned from a trip, and announces that he is leaving you, immediately proceed to step 3. He has already hired his lawyer.

If you have made up your mind that you want the divorce, you may only need steps 2 and 3.

If divorce is a possibility, plan carefully.

Preparing a divorce plan and getting information beforehand is invaluable. Once the battle lines of divorce are drawn, it can be extremely expensive to go through the formal legal process called 'discovery' for information that might be available to you.

DIVORCE PLAN

1 Copy all the bank records, real estate deeds, credit card statements and tax returns you can find. This will help to establish marital standard of living, as well as marital property and debts (see step 8).

2 Some experts will advise women who have joint accounts to withdraw half the money, especially if there is a chance that you will have a hard time getting living expenses from your husband. It is not illegal for you to withdraw money from a joint account; that's what a joint account means. You both own it jointly. Many women who decide to do this, discover that their husband, having planned the divorce in advance, has already taken the money. Some experts, however, say that doing this can disrupt and anger what otherwise might be amicable divorce proceedings. Base your actions on your knowledge of how your husband is likely to react.

3 If you do not have credit in your own name, open charge accounts at department stores and with major credit card companies, while you are still married. If you go out on a spending spree with the cards, however, you could be liable for the debts. If you are just getting married, you do not legally have to change the names on all your charge accounts. You can keep some credit in your own name.

4 If you have children, begin a child care diary, noting who feeds and plays with the children, and who does the laundry. This can be helpful if there is a custody battle.

5 Try to accumulate some cash for expenses for six months and to pay initial legal fees, if possible.

6 Many lawyers advise a woman who can do so to take some courses that will help prepare her for the job market if she is not working—or for a better job if she is.

7 If you have shares, call the broker and find out their value.

8 Be able to document your standard of living. If you and your husband travelled a lot, even though his business paid for it, that is part of your way of life. If you had a car and it was owned by your husband's business, or any other expenses were paid for by your husband's business, include this information. This also helps in determining the value of your husband's business. He may have been charging expenses to the business in order to make the business appear less profitable.

9 Be able to document your non-financial contributions. If you travelled with your husband for his business, be able to explain the business nature of what you did, even if it is something as simple as giving suggestions for a speech he gave. Business consultants charge money for things many wives do automatically. If you actually helped to keep business records, be able to show that too. And this does not apply just to women who are at home. Many highly successful women come home from their own offices to help entertain their husband's business clients. It seldom works the other way, except in TV commercials.

10 Try to establish a list of property that may be your separate property.

11 If you own the business, and it was started with a loan in your name from the bank, or from your uncle Henry, be able to document this.

12 List your outstanding debts. If you have a credit line, find out what property is secured.

13 Some lawyers say that even when fault isn't supposed to count, if it exists, use it. Fault, by the way, doesn't have to mean a picture of your husband with that other woman; it can also mean economic fault. Your husband could have wasted the marital assets. If you can show that he did so, by running up debts to finance a fancy trip for himself, for example, that will be helpful when it comes to dividing the assets because his debts may be counted against his share.

If you don't know what's going on, your husband will have an advantage in negotiating a settlement. He will have a better idea of what assets you have and what they are worth. Despite all your initial hopes that your divorce will be different from those messy ones you've heard about, you may have to fight dirty too. If you think your husband has been hiding assets, you might have to hunt for them.

Some people even hire detectives to ferret out hidden funds, but before you pay out for a private eye, there are a lot of things you can do on your own. If you are feeling squeamish about this, you can buy a lot of information for $30 to $50 an hour. Here's a tip, however, for anyone thinking of hiring a professional. Work through your lawyer. If you hire the detective directly, there is no client/lawyer privilege; your husband's lawyer can demand discovery and get a court order to look at the files. If your lawyer does the hiring, there may be privilege.

HOW TO FIND HIDDEN ASSETS

1. If you want to go the do-it-yourself route, you will need to invest in some equipment. A tape recorder can be invaluable in recording conversations, threats or information about assets that he has well and truly hidden from the eye of the law. But be careful. It is against the law for you to record telephone conversations, even with your husband.

2. A prime source of information is available in your home: the wastepaper basket. Investigate it, you never know what you could find. Possible treasures that could turn up include old cheques that could reveal bank accounts you didn't know about and credit card slips.

3. Check the postmarks on the mail—in fact, check the mail.

4. Illegal cash is tricky. It is illegal. However, many lawyers advise that if you know about illegal cash, you can use this as a negotiating point. Remember, if you know about the 'black economy' money and

you've been signing the tax returns, you could be in trouble too.

5 If you find an unfamiliar key, it may be for a safe deposit box. Try and find out.

6 Your husband's office could be a treasure trove. If you can get inside long enough, copy as many documents as you can find, especially insurance policies, leases and bank statements. *Consult your lawyer, though, to make sure you are not breaking the law.*

BUSINESS RECORDS

If you worked with your husband to build a business, do not assume that it is equally yours and his, unless you can prove it. Show that your money was used, or keep track of the hours you worked. Make sure you are listed as a partner, or an executive. When famed realtor Donald Trump announced that his wife Ivana would become president of New York's Plaza Hotel, Mr Trump announced that her salary would be $1 a year plus all the dresses she could buy. While that may have sounded cute, Mrs Trump would have been better off asking for stock.

> When Rhoda married her husband, who wanted to be an artist, she was earning $50,000 a year. Her husband did odd jobs as a carpenter. Pretty soon, however, he decided to open his own cabinet shop. Rhoda helped finance it, then gave up her job to help in the business in addition to taking care of the books. They pooled their income. But that was all they pooled. Rhoda also did all the housework, while her husband began to play house with a beautiful architect who came in to order shelves for a client. When Rhoda's husband finally left her, Rhoda lost her job, as her husband shut down the business in order to start a new one with his new companion. Rhoda is sure her husband diverted some cash from the old business to the new one, but she can't prove a thing.

It's not unusual for a man to start a business with the help of his wife, who may use her earnings to support the household, or otherwise enable her husband to get started. When the marriage dissolves, it's often the man who keeps the business.

Although most of the divorces that hit the newspapers pit one partner against another, divorces do not have to be like that. There are several routes to divorce.

ROUTES
to DIVORCE

DO IT YOURSELF

There are several books on the market—even a divorce kit. The do-it-yourself divorce is recommended for couples who have few assets, few debts and a very brief marriage, where there is no question of child support or maintenance, and where you each have some sort of superannuation.

If you and your husband have agreed to a divorce, you may be able to choose less adversarial divorce methods. Spouses can apply jointly for divorce. This allows couples who agree that their marriage is over and who have been separated for the required twelve months to dissolve the marriage together. This avoids the need for serving documents. *Settling Up*, the study of how Australians distribute property and income on divorce, includes examples of couples who agreed amicably about the arrangements.

I got nothing. But it was fair because I have much more earning capacity than my ex-wife. She had been my wife for 20 years and brought up the children and I felt I wanted to support her and for her to be comfortable. Also, I left her.[12]

Kathy and her husband divorced after seven years of marriage. She accepted far less than her share—in part because she just wanted out, and partly because she knew that money was important to her husband. 'I knew that my life would improve from the day I left. He would never be happy. At least he now has his money—he can play Silas Marner and count it at night. Leaving was the best thing I ever did.'

Divorce can also be granted 'on the papers'. When there are no children of the marriage under eighteen, judges can grant a divorce on the basis of papers filed in court. The applicant simply has to file and serve on their ex-partner a form called a 'Request to Determine Dissolution Proceedings in the Absence of the Parties'. If at the hearing date the ex-partner has not filed an answer opposing the divorce or a 'Notice Requesting that the Dissolution Not Be Heard in the Absence of the Parties', then neither the applicant nor her lawyer need turn up.

GO TO A COMMUNITY LEGAL CENTRE

You should be in a similar situation as the do-it-yourself group—short marriage, few assets, no children and few debts. This is a little more expensive than doing it yourself, but at least you have someone to ask any questions you want answered. Some centres have computerised systems that generate the required forms as you work through the program.

GO TO A COUNSELLOR OR A MEDIATOR

The Family Court has a free counselling service that offers advice about problems associated with separation or the arrangements you have made for the children. You can ask for separate sessions. You may be required to attend counselling if you and your partner cannot agree about custody or access issues.

MEDIATION

Mediation is the latest buzzword of the divorce profession. As with the do-it-yourself divorce, there are some people more suited to this option than others. Mediation, or alternative dispute resolution (ADR), as it is also called, is an alternative to the traditional court resolution of disputes. A family mediator is a specially trained independent expert who sits down with a husband and wife and helps them come to an agreement. The mediator does not make decisions or give legal advice. Unlike arbitration, where a couple would submit to a binding decision by a third party, a mediator tries to help a couple reach their own agreement. A settlement is not imposed. Mediation can be used to settle the whole divorce or a few sticky issues such as child custody, maintenance or property issues.

Divorce lawyers usually do not like mediation. Lawyers who are not in favour of mediation say that it generally places women at a disadvantage.

I have seen women getting nailed in mediation, particularly when they have an imbalance of power with the spouse. I can give you countless examples of women who are married to high-powered, controlling men, who push mediation because in the mediation sessions they can continue their intimidation and control, where they cannot do that in a litigation setting.[13]

Many lawyers say that mediators who were trained as therapists do not understand the financial complexities of divorce.

Mediation requires the voluntary participation of both husband and wife. If your husband refuses to go to a mediator, you can't go alone.

If you have little knowledge of the family assets, mediation could also be a disaster. One couple who chose mediation, after a twenty-year marriage, were determined to avoid the conflicts they had seen in other divorces. They worked with a mediator to reach an agreement. Throughout their marriage they had always pooled their income, she as a lawyer, he as a stockbroker. During the marriage, money was seldom a problem. They had agreed early on that any money either one would inherit would go directly to their two children.

Their biggest asset was a house. During the real estate boom of the 1980s the value of the home soared to a million dollars. Their other major asset was his superannuation. They had very little in savings, apart from some cash. They agreed that they would split everything and that she would buy out her husband's share of the house. They showed the agreement to a lawyer who prepared the necessary legal documents and took care of the mechanics of the divorce. They decided to take their gross income as a basis for paying a proportionate share of the cost of supporting their two children. Presently, that is one-third for her and two-thirds for her husband. But the wife is hopeful that her income will increase and she will then pay more of her share of the child support.

Cost for the whole process: $2000 to the mediator and $500 to the lawyer. The wife thinks that she might have gotten more money, but she was confident that she would earn money, and she and her husband agreed that they did not want fights about money. Most couples say that, but it doesn't work out that way. Possibly it worked in this case because both parties knew exactly what their assets were and both felt confident of their ability to earn money.

But mediation isn't all good will and positive outcomes. Maggie, a lawyer friend who specialised in mediation, has given it up as a lost cause. A fierce feminist, Maggie says that mediation with a mediator who has no understanding of society's in-built bias in men's favour invariably means an outcome that advantages men.

Women are so conditioned to believe that men are more important, that men's interests are more legitimate, that they agree to compromises that seriously disadvantage them. If you have a mediator who has never really questioned his sexism and his own belief that men are the rightful owners of property (and there are a lot of them), the women don't have a chance.[14]

'A BATTLE to BE WON'

The traditional way of divorcing is to hire a lawyer who guides you through the complicated procedure. Unlike mediation, which tries to bring parties together, the traditional, court battle divorce is an adversarial procedure: you and your husband have different interests, you and your lawyer have different interests, your husband's lawyer and your lawyer have different interests. Like war, it is treated as a battle to be won.

Getting divorced, unlike getting married, is fraught with complex legal questions, as well as emotional reactions. Regardless of your economic situation, whether you work, or have children, the questions you have are likely to be similar to those of other women. Divorce is like any other law suit. There is a plaintiff and a defendant. If you want the divorce and file the papers, you are the plaintiff, and your husband is the defendant.

It's nice to think that the man you married will, if he has supported you in the past, contribute to your support during the divorce negotiations. Sometimes that doesn't happen. You may have to go to court to force your husband to support you.

As far as divorce itself is concerned, the legal process can take a long time. Many lawyers believe that couples need this emotional time in order to get through a divorce. Some lawyers suggest that there is a typical emotional pattern to a divorce. Couples begin by thinking they will be reasonable. Then, somewhere along the line, the situation turns bitter and angry. This, say many lawyers, is a necessary part of the separation process. Others, critical of the adversarial nature of conventional divorces, believe the sometimes hostile negotiations cause the anger.

One matrimonial lawyer, now turned mediator, explains negotiation as follows. Lawyers for opposing parties play a 'game of legal chess', with the object being 'to get as much as you can and give as little as you have to. The rules are that there are no rules.' He believes that frequently lawyers raise clients' expectations, because the lawyers are stating initial bargaining positions, whereas the clients think they are being given final offers. The wife, thinking she has been given a final figure, becomes infuriated, if not insulted, by the paltry offer made by her husband. The husband, who may be the type who measures his self-esteem by his money, has now been asked to part with a huge chunk of what he sees as his hard-earned cash. Naturally, his wife's lawyer doesn't think his client will get that figure. The husband is livid. Never, he says. And the battle is on. Sometimes, it is settled only when the wife realises that she cannot afford to play the game because the lawyer's fees are too high. Sometimes, it is settled only when the husband threatens to go to court, and his wife suspects that he just might and she cannot afford to do so.

Let's assume that you have finally decided that you need a lawyer. Do not walk in and turn your case over to the first lawyer you meet. This is going to be a critical time and it is best to do some research.

TEN QUESTIONS TO ASK BEFORE YOU HIRE A DIVORCE LAWYER

1 **What type of practice do you have—matrimonial, corporate, litigation?**

2 **Do you usually represent men?**

3 **What are the costs?**

If you employ a lawyer acting alone, figures from Queensland show that the costs can be as little as $581 if children under eighteen are involved or $448 if there are no dependants. Lawyers can also ask you to waive these fees and can charge a much higher fee, but only with your approval. And it is tempting to do so if you believe that the particular lawyer you have is a good one. But be careful what you sign. In one notorious case in Sydney in which a Family Court lawyer was disciplined for propounding false documents, the client was not aware at any stage that she had signed a cost agreement varying the minimum fee structure. Almost all of her settlement was taken up with legal fees of $355,174.99.

Your prospective lawyer will also try to assess you, to figure out how much your case will bring in legal fees. You must realise that the longer your case takes, the more money your lawyer can earn.

4 **How will I be billed?**

Billing is extremely important—especially if you do not have much money available because your husband has taken most of it. While some lawyers may work with you without asking for too much up front, if you need appraisers or experts they are expensive and must be paid immediately.

5 **Will my husband pay my fees?**

Many women who do not have separate accounts and money assume that their husbands will pay the legal fees and therefore it is not important to worry about the costs of the divorce. Do not make this assumption. Be very careful, even if your husband offers to pay your legal fees. One lawyer, David W. Belin, recalls learning a lesson when he was just starting his practice. His client was a wealthy man. The lawyer representing the wife was a well-known matrimonial lawyer. Belin's senior partner told him to contest every financial demand made by the wife's solicitor. Except for the fee. That was to be paid. In other words, the wife's lawyer would be willing to settle for less, on behalf of his client, the wife, as long as he knew that his fee would be paid. If at all possible, a wife is better off paying her own fees.

6 Will you require a retainer (money that you give in advance)?

Your lawyer deducts the hourly fee from the retainer until it is used up. Ask to be informed of how much money is being spent.

7 Will you personally handle my case or will I work with an assistant?

8 Will I be able to reach you over the weekend? Or at all?

This is often a serious complaint. Not being able to reach your lawyer on the telephone can be extremely frustrating. One woman who discovered that her husband was moving furniture out of their jointly owned home while she was at work tried, without success, to reach her lawyer. On the other hand, lawyers are understandably protective about their private time, and many tell of calls from clients at all hours of the day and night.

9 Will I need to sign a contract?

If yes, be sure to read it very carefully. It will set out the boundaries of the work your lawyer will do. Be sure to ask about any post-divorce settlement negotiations that may be necessary. One woman found, after she had reached a settlement with her husband, that he refused to turn over the specified property. Her lawyers told her they did not handle any after-divorce proceedings.

10 Will I be given copies of all documents, and will you explain their meaning?

Much of what goes on is the technical filing of motions. Many women complain that they are not told about this by their lawyers.

WAYS to MINIMISE the COST of a DIVORCE

Here are some tips from a top divorce lawyer:

◆ *Don't use your lawyer as a psychiatrist.*
◆ *Have as much information as possible available.*
◆ *Listen to what your lawyer says.*

OTHER MONEY-SAVING TIPS

1. Any time you must call a lawyer on the telephone, have a written list of the questions you want to ask. Then arrange a time to speak with your lawyer. Remember that lawyers usually charge for telephone calls. Most often you will receive a minimum charge of fifteen minutes—whether you speak for five or fifteen minutes, the price will be the same. Wait until you have a few questions before you place your call. Keep a large clock nearby to remind you of the cost.

2. Don't sleep with your lawyer. But if you do, make sure you're not being billed for the time. Urban myth has it that this occurs far more often than is ever acknowledged—perhaps more often than women sleeping with their gynaecologists.

3. Above all, *you have to help manage your case*. You cannot just hire a lawyer and think you are being taken care of by a benevolent mother or father. Remember Rhoda, who didn't keep any records of the money she had put into her husband's business? She made the same mistake when she hired a divorce lawyer. She didn't quiz the lawyer or check his credentials in family law. She didn't query any of the bills, even though costs included huge photocopying bills and one call that she could not possibly have made as she was not in the country at the time. But managing your case means more than watching the legal bills. It means being realistic about when to fight and when to give in. One woman reports that she and her husband had agreed on almost everything, then the lawyers stepped in and she was too frightened to say anything when the lawyer escalated her original demands. She ended up with about the same settlement she had originally expected, but much higher legal fees.

Sometimes, whatever you do, you will not end up with everything you want. Your lawyers can give you a general idea of the way judges are likely to decide various areas of a dispute, should your case go to court. Naturally you would like to avoid that. Once you have hired a lawyer, sit down and talk realistically about your chances.

PROCEED with CAUTION

During the divorce process, you may be making many decisions that seem appropriate at the time, but that you could later regret. The most important decision could be in connection with the family home. Most women want it. But it could be a mixed blessing. For example, if your one asset is a house worth $200,000 and you want to keep it, you would have to come up with some way to give your husband his share of the money. You may end up bargaining away other things to keep the house, only to discover that you can't afford to maintain it. Or you may accept an appraised value of the house that turns out to be too high. When you try to sell the house, you will discover that you have lost money. If you accept the house but rent it out because you can't afford to live in it, you may find yourself paying a hefty capital gains tax when it comes to selling it at a later date. Chances are, the tax payment was not figured into your settlement.

While women at home have lost out when it comes to splitting assets under the new rules of equitable distribution and no-fault divorce, many high-powered career women also discover they have made mistakes that subsequently hurt them. Part of the problem is that the very laws that gave the non-working wife a shot at the marital assets can now be applied to penalise the hard-working woman. Unthinkable as the notion would have been to our grandfathers, men are now demanding, and getting, support from and shares in the businesses of their wives. Lawyers who have dealt with the other side of the coin report that career women are often no more worldly when it comes to protecting themselves than their stay-at-home sisters. And, in those situations where women have been the ones to cough up maintenance and property to their husbands, they have fought as hard as possible against it.

In some cases, mistakes are made right at the beginning of the marriage; others are made even as the marriage begins to deteriorate, and a woman who is otherwise savvy about her career should have known better.

KNOWING WHEN to SETTLE

A big problem in divorce is knowing when to settle. Some 95 per cent of applications other than simply for divorce do not go to trial.[15] Those that do, say many lawyers, are sometimes based on unrealistic expectations. Sometimes these expectations can be fuelled at an early meeting with your lawyer when it is suggested that you should receive a certain settlement. Sometimes, they are brought about by a sense of anger or guilt; or by a feeling of being wronged and therefore wanting what you consider your rights.

The more you understand the financial realities, the more likely you will be to avoid these escalating battles. Often fights develop over an amount of money that, if split, would give each of you more than you will end up giving your lawyers. Yet many couples continue to wage war, ending in a pyrrhic victory for one of them and higher fees for their lawyers.

The emotional scars that these fights can leave may not be worth the struggle—especially since most studies suggest that women are usually happier (and poorer) five years after a divorce than the men from whom they were divorced.

While it is unlikely that you will find yourself in a divorce court, you should know a few things about that. First of all, court cases are very expensive. The hourly fees that you will have to pay your lawyer will add up. In addition, you may have to pay hefty fees to a variety of experts to help prove your point—expert appraisers, if there is a business; experts in stock options, if those exist; and numerous other experts.

If you and your partner are very far apart on what you think you should get, try to estimate what the court expenses might be, plus your other legal fees. Then subtract that amount from what you think you are going to get. Then decide again whether you want the emotional strain of a court battle.

This doesn't mean that you should capitulate on every demand. It just means you don't want to end up dead like the screen couple in *The War of the Roses*.

IMPORTANT QUESTIONS TO ASK
ABOUT YOUR CASE

1 **What are the general rules about property division?**
When settling property, the court looks at what the parties have contributed to acquiring and maintaining assets, and the ability of each to maintain themselves. A wife's contribution as homemaker and parent is considered. The parent who takes the children usually receives a compensatory share of the property. Repartnering of a woman is often seen as 'reducing' her need. The reality exposed in studies, such as *Settling Up* in 1986, is that the car (or the best of two cars) goes to the husband. Other assets and financial resources owned individually are usually retained by the person who used them during the marriage. Men kept their boats, tools and sporting equipment; women kept their jewellery. Superannuation, although usually of sufficient value to make a difference to property division, is rarely divided so that both partners have an equitable share. Debts and liabilities, even when taken out by one partner without the knowledge of the other, can be the responsibility of both. This is especially unfair when the debt is incurred between separation and settlement. Little of the above bodes well for women.

2 *What are the laws about maintenance?*

Spouse maintenance is usually only offered where a wife is unable to support herself. In the case of child maintenance, all parents, whether married or not, are responsible for the financial support of their children. Agreements should be registered with the Child Support Agency.

3 *How are superannuation and life insurance policies dealt with?*

There are issues about how these are valued and how they can be 'paid' when they are not due to vest for many years. They should always be considered as part of the settlement.

4 *How is the family home likely to be divided?*

The person who leaves the family home on separation is most unlikely to obtain it on distribution of property. Only if there are considerable other assets is it likely that the family home will not have to be sold. Ironically, while many decisions about the family home are made with the idea that it will provide a secure environment for the children, a study in 1986 showed that 43 per cent of children left the matrimonial home on separation; 67 per cent had left within three years and 77 per cent had left within five years.

5 *Is standard of living an issue?*

Partners of long-standing marriages should expect to maintain their standard of living as far as is possible under the circumstances. This is likely to be effected through the property settlement rather than through long-term maintenance.

6 *Hidden assets*

If you believe that your partner is transferring assets, tell your lawyer, who may be able to get an injunction prohibiting your husband from moving the assets out.

RETIREMENT?
FOR WHOM?

'RETIREMENT? WE'LL NEVER BE able to retire.' Carol, aged forty-three, and her husband Peter, aged fifty, have a ten-month old baby. Carol, a computer programmer, has recently stopped work in order to spend time with her baby. Peter is manager of a store and has never earned as much as Carol. Now, as they try to live on Peter's salary, retirement seems remote, if not impossible.

This is a big change from earlier centuries. In the early Middle Ages, average life expectancy was forty-five years, but for women it was only thirty to forty years. There were few old people and little need to plan or provide for retirement.

By the time of the Industrial Revolution, wealthy landowners were expected to take care of their peasants and factory workers. If the workers were lucky enough not to die from accidents or injuries at work, they went to a poor house or to the old age home. There was no system of paying money directly to the elderly or the sick. Otto von Bismarck introduced old age pensions in Germany in the 1880s, as part of his program of state socialism: not as a liberal measure but to forestall democratic socialism. Bismarck thought the ideal retirement age was sixty-five.[1] By coincidence, that was the average life expectancy of the German worker.

For Australians, life expectancy has far surpassed that of the German worker of 1880. Today, women can expect to live into their eighties and men into their late seventies.

Retirement age under the Social Security system is sixty-five for men and, currently, sixty for women. Along with other changes to the Social Security system, the retirement age for women is gradually to be raised to sixty-five.

THE IMPORTANCE of PLANNING

For women, even retiring at sixty-five means that they have still fifteen years on average to live—without an income from paid work. And for women over sixty-five, 30 per cent will be widowed, either living with their families, on their own (37 per cent), or in some form of shared or supported accommodation.[2] By the time they turn eighty-five, three-quarters of Australian women will be widowed and responsible for their own financial well-being. And let's face it, being a bag lady at eighty-five is hardly a prospect to be relished.

If you consider that, statistically, most women will be on their own for their last ten years or so, the financial provisions made for retirement are vitally important. Remember that inflation, even at 5 per cent, will double the cost of everything in fourteen years. This means that if you outlive your husband by the expected average, your expenses will double during the time you are alone.

Clearly, the worker who invests early on and lets money accumulate in some sort of retirement plan has a great advantage over the worker who starts later or who takes time out.

$1000 invested at 6 per cent can grow:
- *after ten years you would have $1790.*
- *after twenty years you would have $3210.*

In 1992:

◆ approximately 30 per cent of women over the age of sixty-five were widowed.

◆ over 80 per cent of all widowed persons were women.

◆ 73 per cent of women aged eighty-five and over were widowed.[3]

For the generation now in their forties or younger, planning for retirement is more important than ever before. Even their parents had it easier. Most had their children young and in an economy that continued to grow through the 1950s and '60s. For most, the kids were off their hands by the time the parents were in their late forties. They had twenty child-free years in which to accumulate wealth and plan for their retirement.

The reality is that the present crop of older Australians—now in their sixties and seventies—regard themselves as being a peculiarly lucky generation . . . Their life expectancy was dramatically stretched by the new development of antibiotics, by the new enlightenment about heart disease and the giant strides in surgery that have occurred in the last quarter of this century.

Now they look around them and feel luckier still. Seeing the new difficulties being faced by their children's generation—to say nothing of the bleak employment prospects of their grandchildren—they heave a sigh of relief that they made it to retirement with their marriages, their careers and their values intact.[4]

But it is a different scene for the forties and under. This is the generation who are faced with more of their offspring going on to tertiary studies and with more children staying at home longer. Their children are likely to be dependent for a longer time and to return home in need of financial support. This is the generation who had their kids later—with the result that many parents still have completely dependent children when they are contemplating retirement. And they are part of a generation where only 53 per cent will still be together after thirty years. Separation, death or divorce will affect the other 47 per cent. So, early planning for retirement—with contingency plans—is a must. This means knowing about your money and your partner's. It means making the effort to plan around pensions, superannuation and investments.

SOCIAL SECURITY

If you rely only on the age pension (currently $8221 a year) you are courting poverty. And if you rely on a partner's financial assets instead of making your own plans, you may be one of the many over sixty-fives who end up living below the poverty line.

Social Security in the form of the age pension is available to men over sixty-five and, currently, women over sixty, although from 1 July 1995 women's eligibility will gradually be changed so that they too must be sixty-five to receive the age pension. Payment is subject to an asset and income test. To receive the full pension (July 1994), single home owners must have assets under $115,000, not including the home they live in, and can have up to $223,000 in assets before the pension cuts out. Married couples have an asset limit of $163,500 for the full pension and a limit of $338,000 before they become ineligible. Pension rates, again at July 1994, are $323.30 per fortnight for single people and $267.90 each per fortnight for couples. These amounts include a small pharmaceutical allowance. With some particular variations and bits and pieces that apply to certain investments and rollover funds, a single person can earn $90 per fortnight and married couples $156 per fortnight combined. These rates are indexed to the CPI and increase slightly for each additional dependent child. For every $1 of income above the free area, the pension reduces by 50 cents.

A recent AMP survey[5] showed that 85 per cent of retirees

enjoy being retired, but two out of three said their living expenses were at least the same as before they retired. More than a quarter said their living expenses had increased. The couple whose pre-retirement income was $50,000 should therefore not expect to maintain anything like the same standard of living on half that amount. And don't think that you can retire graciously on the pension. It may be enough to keep the wolf from the door, but it certainly doesn't provide enough for even one little pig to live in warmth and comfort inside. Says Belle, sixty-two, whose husband retired two years ago at sixty-five:

We saved for our retirement and invested the money, assuming we would live off the interest. When interest rates plummeted we found we had to keep using the capital. Retirement isn't cheaper—not if you want to enjoy life after working for fifty years as my husband did. We had trouble at first. I had to get used to not buying magazines and little things like hand cream and new stockings. We have to budget for petrol and there are no more dinners out at fancy restaurants. It's the Leagues Club now. A group of us meet there on Tuesday nights— pensioners night—and can have a meal for under $10 each. It's a far cry from the life we lived before retirement. I have to say it was a bit hard to get used to.[6]

Belle also talks about some of her women friends, most of whom are widowed. One, who had her own business, is quite well off, has a car and travels overseas each year. The others are all in varying states of genteel poverty. 'They all keep up appearances,' she says, 'but they can't even afford the $10 for the club on Tuesday nights. The only ones who can are three of them who live together. But I don't know if it's worth it. They don't get on very well. You know, after living in your own home for forty years, it's hard to share with someone else who has different ways of doing things.'

Obviously many retirees have either found it too expensive

or too boring to retire. One-quarter of Sydney's over fifty-fives who have retired are in paid work. The latest Australian Bureau of Statistics figures establish that 8.5 per cent of men and 2.5 per cent of women over sixty-five are in paid employment.[7]

If your partner dies, you may be entitled to certain benefits. A widow is classified as someone legally married at the time of her husband's death, or divorced from her husband, or not legally married but living with and dependent on her partner for three years immediately before his death. She can also be a woman who is married to a man who was continuously in prison for six months, or be a legally married women who has either left her husband or been left for a period of six months.[8]

CATEGORIES of WIDOW'S PENSION

There are three categories of widow's pension (Classes A, B and C). To qualify for a Class A pension, a woman must be maintaining a dependent child and also have a 'qualifying child'—that is, a dependent child under sixteen years of age who is either the natural child of the woman or was being maintained by the woman when she became a widow. Once her last 'qualifying child' turns sixteen, she is no longer eligible for the Class A pension, even if she is still supporting other children.

To be eligible for a Class B widow's pension you must be a widow and have been:

♦ *receiving a widow's pension (Class B) before 1 July 1987,*
♦ *over the age of fifty on 1 July 1987 and were subsequently widowed, or*

♦ *over forty-five years of age at 1 July 1987 and either then or at some future time received a sole parent's payment—or an equivalent payment.*

Obviously this pension is being phased out. Those who no longer qualify have to apply for other benefits or pensions, such as the age pension, or seek employment.

The Class C widow's pension is paid to a legally married woman, or one who was dependent on a man for three years before his death, who is under fifty years of age, has no dependent children and is in need of financial assistance. The pension can be paid for twenty-six weeks after a partner's death.

Even if you are one of the relatively few who still qualifies for a widow's pension, you are not likely to be living even as well as Belle. And superannuation and life insurance, while it may help, is not going to make most of us rich, as a study into the situation of widows with children has shown:

It makes little difference whether they are widowed or divorced. Widowed mothers may receive life insurance or superannuation payments, divorced mothers may receive maintenance. The reality is that most receive neither. The majority of widowed families . . . particularly those headed by a woman, were living on extremely low incomes, as are most divorced or separated female parents.[9]

SUPERANNUATION

Ten years ago the Australian government realised that with the ageing population the bill for maintaining the elderly on the pension was going to be prohibitive. Simply, there would not be enough people of working age to create the money to pay for the care and maintenance of the old.

With this in mind, in 1992 the Superannuation Guarantee Charge Levy on employers was introduced by the federal government. The levy is currently at 5 per cent (3 per cent for small employers) and is due to rise to 9 per cent in 2000.

The scheme is eventually to provide employees with 40 per cent of their working income when they retire, in return for 12 per cent of their wages today—this, of course, for those who are aged fifteen at the moment. Everyone else will get much less than 40 per cent. A similar scheme is mooted for self-employed people by 1996.

If you are wealthy and have a personal superannuation scheme, you can pay far more than the minimum required by the government. If you can arrange your life so as to be a judge, for example (on about $170,000 a year), you can retire on 60 per cent of your income without having made any contributions and still command $2000 a day. Unfortunately, this is not an option for most women.

Under the current superannuation scheme, a fifty-five year old in 1994 who earns $750 a week will have $23,487 in ten years when they retire, and it may be that this will have to be paid in the form of an annuity of 5 per cent of the lump sum— that is about $23 a week. A forty-five year old on $1250 a week is looking at a lump sum after tax of $117,552 and an annuity of $119 a week. For those in their fifties this means that superannuation will provide about 3 per cent of pre-retirement income; their main source of income will be the pension. Not until the current twenty-year olds are receiving their superannuation pay-outs will they have anything like the 40 per cent pre-retirement income to live on.

In 1991, 65.5 per cent of employed women had superannuation cover, compared with 75.3 per cent of employed men. However, as women earn, overall, 61 per cent of male earnings, their contribution to a superannuation package will be far less. And as just over 50 per cent of women are in the paid work force, that leaves a lot of women without cover for the future.

When it comes to superannuation, despite all the books that speak about you and your spouse, for women the future can seem bleak. The higher wages and longer years of work that men experience and the lower wages and interrupted work years of most women culminate, not surprisingly, in fewer benefits when they retire. Indeed, the mean income for women in 1989/90 was $14,000 a year. (New South Wales figures in the Australian Bureau of Statistics National Census of 1991 put the median annual income for women at $23,740.) Paying into a superannuation fund on that basis, at 3 per cent a year, would yield an annual contribution of $420 a year. With charges and commissions, it would take years to accumulate even $1000 to collect on retirement.

Women frequently drop out of the work force to raise children. For this reason, or because they often change jobs, they end up with less money than men. Also, according to a 1993 survey by the Australian Bureau of Statistics, women were more likely to opt out of superannuation schemes than men because their husbands were covered by a scheme. One in five women with superannuation cover still expected to be dependent on someone else's income in retirement.

As we have seen, though, it is not wise for women to rely on a partner's income or superannuation in retirement. Access to their superannuation can be lost through divorce or death. In the latter case, more than a few women who have assumed that they were the beneficiaries of their partner's superannuation have been shocked to find that someone else has been named. Husbands in second marriages often want to leave something to the children from their first—and this may be at the second wife's expense.

As family law practitioner Kim Ford stated in a *Sydney Morning Herald* article:

Women for so long have relied on their spouse's super to provide their retirement income. That is why many women tend to do a lot worse in divorce then men. They rely on the man to be around to provide their retirement income, and when they divorce that financial security isn't there any more.[10]

If you do divorce, superannuation policies are considered financial assets of the marriage and should be taken into account at the divorce settlement. The Family Court has used two main approaches to dividing superannuation.[11]

1. One approach is to treat it as a financial resource that is taken into account when calculating the property division. This means the court takes it into account and considers this in a general way when deciding how to split the assets. The partner without the superannuation would receive more of the assets of the marriage at the time of the divorce on the understanding that the holder of the superannuation will get (usually) his or her rewards when the superannuation is paid out.

2. The other approach is more specific and treats the superannuation as part of the property of the marriage. It is valued and divided between the couple after their contributions to the marriage and future needs have been assessed. In effect, the party with the superannuation retains it and the other party gets a sort of compensatory order. The problem is that if the superannuation is the main asset, there may be no other assets to provide the compensation.

The Family Court has sometimes held over judgment until the superannuation 'vests'—that is, becomes payable. The court either makes a deferred property order requiring a fixed proportion to be paid, or adjourns the proceedings until the superannuation benefits are payable. This means you could be waiting for years for a payout.

In assessing the current value of a policy that may not be

due to vest for many years, the court has either worked out the amount of benefit if the member resigned so that future payments are not considered, or has calculated how much payments to the scheme will be worth on retirement and then discounted that amount to its present net value.

Neither of these methods is ideal. An alternative is to adopt a system similar to that in New Zealand where, on divorce, the court can require the trustee of a superannuation fund to split the fund in two, giving each spouse a continuing interest with a separate trust deed for each spouse.

For couples contemplating retirement, adequate superannuation will take much of the fear of poverty out of old age. Unless one of you becomes very sick over a long period and has enormous healthcare bills not covered by Medicare, you will probably be able to live comfortably in a material sense. But there are other issues to consider.

Generally speaking, it is still the case that superannuation is in the husband's name. The wife is either not working or has far less in the way of superannuation entitlements. This means the husband is in a position to have more of a say in retirement planning. This may suit some, but many women want to be in a position to have at least an equal say. You may have a very different attitude towards spending money in retirement when you realise that you will probably outlive your husband by up to fifteen years. What you both spend will not be there for you during all those years alone.

It can also mean that the superannuation may not be available if you split up—and it is not uncommon for older couples to do this after retirement. Forty years of living together amicably while you each have paid work and your own interests is quite different from the prospect of at least fifteen years sharing the same space, 24 hours a day, and with a husband who takes over running the house to compensate for no longer running a business!

LIFE INSURANCE

Before superannuation became popular, many of those who were careful enough to plan ahead took out life insurance. Many people still do. Life insurance is a way of protecting people's interests in themselves and others. By taking out a life insurance policy—on your own or your partner's life—you are protecting yourself and your family financially from the adverse effects of your or their death.

It is undoubtedly true with insurance policies that you pay for what you get. Finding the policy that best suits you may involve some shopping around so that you have a real understanding of what is being offered and how much it will cost you. Sometimes, on badly structured policies, you can pay a lot more than you get. Policies vary from company to company and within companies, but basically you pay premiums over a period of time, and when the insured person dies the company pays out the agreed amount.

A friend's father, who had been sick for some time, died earlier this year. His life was insured and his widow made a claim on the insurance company. To her dismay, the claim was refused on the grounds that her husband had the illness from which he died *before* he took out his policy and had not disclosed this. Shocked, she contacted a lawyer who instructed her to challenge the decision. She was able to provide evidence from the family doctor that the illness was not 'pre-existing' and the insurance company paid up without further queries.

On divorce, policy holders usually hold on to their policies, which are not always taken into account in property settlements because partners don't think to include them. When they are accounted for, they can be surrendered and the surrender value of the policy can be used as a source of cash on distribution of the assets. This can solve a problem where the former spouse was named as beneficiary under the policy.

CONTINGENCY PLANS —
DEATH, DISMISSAL
or DISABILITY

Your pension entitlements will change if your partner dies. For eligible pensioners, there is a small lump sum payable to the surviving spouse. Where a surviving spouse is not eligible for a sole parent pension, there is a pension available for a period of twelve weeks from the death of a partner. Carer's pensions are available for seven days after the death of a partner for whom the pensioner has been caring. To find out what your benefits will be, call the number for the Department of Social Security listed in the phone book.

For most women, there is an ever looming problem. Inflation will erode the purchasing power of your retirement income. In addition, when you are widowed, which is likely, your income will drop. Unfortunately, for most women, it is the husband, who has the larger pension, who is likely to die sooner. Remember, the average woman outlives her husband by at least fifteen years; if inflation is only 4 per cent, a $6 movie in a few years will cost closer to $12.

Frequently, women just do not think about their finances for retirement. Often women will say, 'I think my husband has made provision for retirement but I'm not sure of the details.' Many women abdicate their role in planning for their own retirement. This is a legacy of the traditional belief that men will provide and take care of women. It is the reason many women in their thirties, who are not yet married, do not start any kind of savings plan at all. They succumb to the old belief that they will marry and be taken care of.

The 1990s began with a recession the effects of which are still being felt. It is not unusual to pick up the paper and read headlines about large companies that have laid off hundreds of people. Yet, few people are prepared for the financial dislocation this can cause. Of course, there is severance pay, usually tied to the length of time you have worked for the company. And, depending on the size of the company, there may be such 'perks' as out-placement services and even the use of an office for a period of time.

These days, if you and your partner work, it is he who is likely to lose his job, especially if he is in middle management.

Both of you have to consider what would happen to your finances if either of you were out of work for an extended period of time. When you lose your job, expenses don't really change that much. In fact, the expenses of finding another job may increase your expenditure.

For many men in their early fifties, dismissal is really a form of early retirement. Financial planners report seeing men in their late fifties who planned to work until age sixty-five now forced out of their jobs, with little chance of finding a comparable position.

There is another possible problem that many couples will face—that of disability. Sometimes, whatever you do, the unforeseen will arise. While it is hard to be prepared for every one of life's blows, there are a few that can be softened. One possibility is to take out a form of disability insurance that provides you with a percentage of your income while the insured person is unable to work. Most reputable insurers have disability policies that offer benefits according to your contributions over time. Do your research carefully. One couple were devastated to discover that the husband's disability insurance policy covered only his regular salary and not the bonus that he thought was part of his yearly earnings.

When Mary Green's husband was sixty, he suffered a stroke. She was suddenly plunged into a world of hospitals, doctors and therapists. As time elapsed and the expenses continued to mount, she had to hire nurses around the clock. She spent a lot of money on therapy, but her husband never regained his faculties. He can sit in a chair and he can walk. He can even play pool. But he can't remember how to keep score.

Because Mary's husband had the stroke before his sixty-fifth birthday, he was forced to retire with less than maximum superannuation benefits. He did not have disability insurance, and money became a problem. Income was not sufficient to cover expenses.

After some research, Mary found a solution. She sold their house and moved to a retirement village.

SUPPORTED ACCOMMODATION

Retirement villages are not a cheap or risk-free solution to your problems. You pay a lot to enter, and then pay high monthly fees for services that can include meals, nursing care and hospital availability.

Retirement villages are generally run by church or charitable organisations, or by commercial organisations for profit. Usually, residents pay a significant amount to buy into the village and then pay regular service charges. To be well-looked after in pleasant, comfortable surroundings, you are talking of $100,000 entry and $200 a week. There are, of course, enormous variations on this. Some supported accommodation/care facilities offer nursing care and reasonable surroundings for the equivalent of the age pension. Others, operating like boarding houses, may take the residents' pensions—and more—and offer sub-standard care and facilities. If you are considering a retirement village or nursing home, make sure that you spend some time looking at the range of options. Having chosen the most likely, spend some time wandering around and talking to the residents and staff.

In New South Wales more than 6 per cent of people over fifty-five live in supported accommodation—that is, they receive some sort of care (nursing) and/or services (meals) in self-care units or hostels in retirement villages or nursing homes. Figures from 1986, undoubtedly much higher now, showed that 82,260 people were in nursing homes in Australia. Of those 72.6 per cent were women, many of them widows. Most of these women probably cared for their partners during a final illness, leaving themselves with a reduced income and few assets.

FINANCIAL PLANNING for RETIREMENT

One way to plan for retirement is to visit a financial planner. The cost can range from a few hundred to a few thousand dollars, depending on the complexity of your assets. Or you can do it yourself with a work book or plan. There are popular computer programs that you can use. If you don't know much about your retirement plans and your husband doesn't like to talk about it—because he doesn't like to think about retiring— suggesting that you visit a planner might be a great idea. Often a concerned wife brings her husband to a planner. Many planners will not see a husband without his wife, or a wife without her husband. Word of mouth and company recommendations are good ways to find a planner. Remember, however, that this is an unlicensed field; just about anyone can hang up a financial planning sign. Financial planners generally work in one of two ways. One group charges a fee and does not sell products. The other group is usually affiliated with a company, either insurance or brokerage or tax shelter, and offers free advice hoping to recoup on the products you subsequently buy.

Financial planning really forces you to focus on facts. The planning process can also bring out some hidden conflicts. Some of the problems are the recurrent financial fights in a marriage—you want to spend money on curtains, your husband wants to spend money on a wine cellar. But often deeper conflicts are revealed. One planner told of a husband who didn't want to have life insurance for his wife, because he didn't 'want some other man spending his money'. Sometimes, when a wife begins her career later in life than her husband, especially if she is a few years younger than him, she may not want to retire at all, preferring to continue working.

How much money you actually have, how much money you will need for retirement and how you will get there, are the basic questions of the planning business. Computers make it easy to project a series of numbers in order to find out how much income you will need when you retire. But working with a planner means you have to understand the assumptions behind the plan.

While there are more scientific ways to figure out how much income you will need in order to retire, here are some guidelines. You will probably need 70 per cent of the average of the last three years of your pre-retirement income. Some of this may come from savings and investments or from retirement superannuation. Planners use a rate of inflation and a rate of interest to figure out how much money you will need when you retire. They also use actuarial tables to estimate how many years you can expect to live.

You should know what those assumptions are, in order to evaluate any advice you get.

There are several problems with financial planning. Most financial plans cannot take into account the likelihood of inflation eroding your standard of living, because the plan never projects an increase in income while you are retired. If inflation is 7 per cent, purchasing power will erode by half in just ten years. Nor does the plan usually project, as has happened in the early 1990s, a precipitous drop in interest rates. When this happens, projected income fails to materialise. Social Security does give you a cost of living increase, but to limit your retirement plans to Social Security when you can make additional arrangements is short-sighted.

The second problem is that the plan changes when one of you dies. The early retirement years will probably be shared. But you also need the contingency plans for disability, death, dismissal or divorce.

Many women still think they do not have to plan for their own retirement, because their husband will provide for them. When it comes to pensions, savings and other plans for the future, every woman should know what her partner has, and should plan for her own future as well.[13]

QUESTIONS TO ASK
A FINANCIAL PLANNER:

1. What is the assumed rate of inflation?

2. What is the assumed rate of growth in assets?

3. What is the assumed yield?

4. Does the plan include spending assets?

5. Is the income taxable?

6. How do 'rollovers' work?

It is 1995. You visit a financial planner. Your husband would like to retire in eleven years. You both feel that if you had an annual income of $50,000 (70 per cent of your current $70,000 income) you would be okay. The financial planner does a bit of calculating and determines that in the year 2006, you would need $89,793. You gasp. Instead of gasping, ask what the assumed rate of inflation is. You are told the inflation rate is 5 per cent. Lately inflation has been low, but think back and remember what inflation was like a few years ago. Then ask the planner to tell you what would happen if inflation was higher or lower. The following chart illustrates what the change in numbers can mean for that $50,000.

	INFLATION		
	3%	5%	9%
YOUR $50,000 RETIREMENT INCOME IN 2006 DOLLARS	$71,288	$89,793	$140,633

The planner looks at the amount of money you have stashed away in savings and superannuation, and tells you that in order to get that $89,793 in the year 2006, you would need a nest egg of $1.8 million if you could be assured of a 6 per cent yield. But if you knew you could get 10 per cent you would only need $1.1 million. The amount you have already saved will then be subtracted from the amount you will need. The planner will then suggest several ways to close the gap. You can decide you will manage on less. You can increase the amount of money you are putting away. You can decide that you will sell your house and invest that money, assuming you can rent for less money than you could make by investing the proceeds from the sale of your house. You can decide that you will spend assets. This is known as spending down. You start with a fixed sum and then withdraw a certain amount each year, until you are left with zero. For example, if you started with $50,000 and withdrew $580 each month, your money would last for ten years.[12]

WILL POWER

BRETT WHITELEY, ONE OF Australia's more revered artists, died in June 1992 from a drug overdose. As well as a substantial estate, he left a daughter, a former wife, a de facto and many wills, some of which seemed to have disappeared. His daughter, Arkie, claimed that as well as the last will found, he had made informal wills, one of which he had taped underneath the fourth drawer of the kitchen cabinet. That will left most of his estate to her. Unfortunately, after his death that will was missing—although the tape remained.

Whiteley's de facto wife first argued that he had given her a handwritten piece of paper in May 1991 that really was his last will. She then changed her mind and accepted the last will found. This left certain pieces of work to what was to become the Brett Whiteley Museum and gave her one-tenth of the remainder of the estate. Arkie said that that will was a device to prevent her mother getting the paintings, which were regularly sold for six-figure sums.

The judge believed the daughter, whose story was supported by Whiteley's accountant's recollection of the contents of the will that was no longer taped to the drawer. The judge said the mere fact that the will cannot be found doesn't mean that it can't take precedence over a will that is actually in existence. Accordingly, it was held that the missing will had indeed existed, and its contents were as told to the court.

As a result, the accountant with the good memory and the artist's daughter were named as executors. Whiteley's mother got $500,000, while the de facto got one painting. A scholarship was established, a school got one painting and the daughter received the rest of the substantial estate. The Brett Whiteley Museum, and arguably the public, lost out, as did the former wife.

The Whiteley Estate is the exception to the usual proposition that wills bring certainty to our last wishes. They are supposed to ensure that your worldly goods go—or do not go—to particular people.

The oldest known will is that of Uah, an Egyptian who lived in the third millennium BC. Australian wills, like many of our marital customs, derive from the Anglo-Saxon tradition. One of the earliest English wills on record was written by a wealthy woman named Wolgith, in the 11th century. Evidently a woman of considerable property, she divided up her vast estates between her numerous children and her church. And offered up a solemn curse to anyone who tried to contest her wishes.

Anyone over the age of eighteen years can make a will. If you don't leave a will, your property, known as your 'estate', passes to your next of kin in a particular order according to the rules of intestacy. If you have no children but a spouse or de facto spouse, that person will receive the whole of the estate. If there are children, the situation is more complicated and depends upon the size of the estate. If it exceeds $100,000, the spouse or de facto gets the first $100,000, household effects and half of the remaining estate: the children take the other half. There are special rules that govern occupation of the matrimonial home. If there are no partners or children, the parents will inherit, and in their absence, relatives will get a windfall.

If there is a will, a surviving de facto has some rights that may have to be taken into account in distributing the deceased's estate. If you are not satisfied with the will left by your partner, you can challenge it in some circumstances.

You might want to claim it is not valid. In one quite significant case, the family of an elderly man who had been in hospital for some time challenged his will on the grounds that it had been made under the influence of one of the nursing staff. Just weeks before he died, he had changed his will and left everything to one of the nurses who had been looking after him. The court agreed with the family and adjusted the will accordingly.

Like Arkie Whiteley, you may believe and be able to prove that the existing will was not the last will, or that the will-maker didn't have the mental capacity to make it. Further, you might be able to take advantage of laws like the *Family Provisions Act 1983* (NSW), the purpose of which is to correct unjust or unfair treatment of relations or dependants who have been left without proper provision being made for them. As spouse or de facto you might be able to successfully claim that the will failed to make proper provision for your maintenance, education or advancement in life.

In deciding whether you or the children received your fair share, the court would take into account the will-maker's character and conduct and that of others—such as the nurse who was named the beneficiary of the elderly man she looked after in hospital. Any contribution you made towards his property or welfare would also be considered—for example, you may have abandoned your own work to care for the will-maker during a long illness.

Many couples think they do not need a will if everything is owned in joint names. This is true, up to a point. However, as mentioned above, it gets more complicated if it is a big estate and there are children. But what happens if you both die in an accident? When a couple dies at the same time and the time of death of each cannot be distinguished, the law in most states presumes that the oldest died first. The estates are then distributed on that basis.

You may also think you do not need a will because you have property that will not be part of your estate. For example, insurance policies and retirement benefits can be paid to your beneficiaries and do not become part of your estate. Having a will allows for unlikely contingencies as well. You probably will not die with a winning lottery ticket in your pocket, but what if you do?

Married women have been known not to have wills, on the basis that their husband has a will that will 'look after' them. Whether this is from ignorance or a sense that they have no right to assume ownership of marital assets, it is not a sensible decision. If, as in the case above, they and their husband die in a car accident at the same time, it would be assumed that the older (husband) died first. If his will left everything to her and she had no will, she would be considered as dying intestate. This means that the estate would be divided according to law and not according to any plans she and her husband may have made.

Many assets now pass outside people's wills because they are disposed of by contracts or other agreements. Only property that you own can be put in your will. If you and your husband own your house jointly, you inherit the house if your husband dies first. His share of the house does not have to be left to you in his will. And, if the house is in joint names, he can't leave his half to anyone else.

Laws relating to wills differ slightly from state to state. If you divorce in New South Wales, any gifts left to a former spouse are cancelled—unless there is evidence from the will-maker that he or she did not intend the will to be revoked. For example, if your ex-husband re-signs his will *after* you divorce, then it will be taken by the courts to still be valid. In New

South Wales, divorce also cancels any appointment of a former spouse as executor or trustee and generally treats a former spouse as if she or he died before the person who made the will.

The same is not true in other states, where second families can get a very rude shock if a will made during a first marriage has never been changed. In one case, a family found that their father had left everything to his first wife whom he had divorced thirty years before and to whom he had never spoken since. Check what rules apply in your state when you make a will.

A will allows you to have the last word. When Paul Getty, the American oil executive and multi-millionaire, died, he left his villa in Italy to three of his girlfriends: one had the right to redecorate, one had the right to supervise the servants, and apparently all three had the right to live in it at the same time. Getty knew this would anger all three of the women.

Sometimes, you might want to be sure that a favourite, but not necessarily valuable, possession is in good hands. Such items can be included in the will, or if there are too many, then list them in a separate letter detailing the personal property that you would like to give to friends or relatives. This cuts down on legal costs.

WHY HUSBANDS AND WIVES SHOULD EACH HAVE WILLS

1. Wills let you give your property away as you wish. But only up to a point. See the comments above on the *Family Provisions Act*.

2. A will lets you name an executor—the person who is responsible for carrying out the terms of the will. If no executor is named in the will, an administrator will be appointed by the court. A solicitor may be appointed, but that person is entitled to be paid for their professional services as an executor.

3. A will is the place where you can name a guardian and make financial provisions for under-age children. If you do not name a guardian and there is some argument about who will be the guardian, the state will appoint one. Many couples report that the naming of a guardian for young children is one of the biggest problems they face. Of course, you can also use your will to disinherit your children, remembering that they may challenge it if they think it unfair.

4. If you have children and die without a will, they will inherit any money outright, usually when they are eighteen and subject to the intestacy rules mentioned above. Some children can deal with a windfall— others might not. Lawyers report that children have embarked on great sprees, spending all their inheritance on cars, boys or girls, and drugs by the time they are twenty-five.

5. Your estate will save expenses if a court-appointed administrator is not needed. If you do not have a will and the next of kin wants to obtain letters of administration which attest to the validity of the will, documents need to be filed in the court. Unless consent can be obtained from all next of kin to dispense with the administration bond, the applicant must lodge with the court a sum of money and a guarantee (bond) that she or he will carry out their functions properly.

6. Without a will it may take longer for the assets to be distributed.

M E N   w i t h o u t   a   W I L L

Many men are reluctant to think about a will, let alone write one. Psychiatrists have long equated the reluctance to write a will with fear of death.[1] Pablo Picasso, who was ninety-one when he died on 8 April, 1973, did not leave a will. In fact, he seems to have taken delight in predicting that the settling of his estate 'will be worse than anyone imagines'. The wrangling over his US$260 million estate lasted almost four years. Eventually his assets were divided between his wife, his children and his grandchildren. The Government of France was given a large share of his paintings, instead of death taxes. Lawyers' fees consumed a huge chunk of the assets.

Writing a will means having to admit one's mortality. It also means having to think about giving up control of one's assets. Some men are simply superstitious. They think writing a will might hasten their death.

Sometimes, men don't want to talk about a will, because they then have to reveal how they value their property versus their wife and children. Recently, a friend's husband died. They owned their home as tenants in common, which meant they could each name an heir for their share. He left his half to his children. And they wanted their money. So, in addition to her grief, the widow had to confront her anger. Anger that he could have done this to her. He obviously felt that 'It's just a house'. But she felt that it was her home and that she had been betrayed.

For men there is an added problem. Those same statistics that tell us that women will outlive their husbands, by fifteen or so years, are reminders to husbands that their wives will go on without them. Some men can contemplate this with reasonable humour, many cannot.

It would be nice to think that all partners were as generous as American multi-millionaire Vincent Astor. His widow recalled him saying, 'You're going to have a good time when I'm gone.'[2] On his death, she became head of a foundation worth millions of dollars. Mrs Astor has used the money to become one of New York City's greatest art patrons.

While you might suggest that your partner write a will, sometimes all of the reasons you can give are not enough to make him do it.

Sometimes you can push too hard, and then the will won't count. At least, that is what happened to Jean Gerard. Ms Gerard, a former Ambassador to Luxembourg and a bigwig in the American Republican Party, inherited US$10 million from her husband, James Gerard. There was only one problem. Gerard signed the will, in his hospital bed, only nine days before he died of bone cancer. Gerard's previous will, written four months earlier, had left nothing outright to his wife; in fact, he had left 40 per cent of his assets in trust for her, the balance of his estate having been left in trusts for his two children. After hearing thirty-five witnesses, the judge ruled that Ms Gerard had unduly influenced her husband, who was in no condition to think about such things.

WOMEN and WILLS

Little has been written about women's attitudes towards making wills. One reason for this may be that women have seldom, in the past, made their own money. Until the *Married Women's Property Act 1879* (NSW) was passed, even if they did earn their own money, their husbands owned it. When they inherited substantial amounts, it was usually left in such a way that the women had little control over where the money would go after they died.

There is no formal requirement that a solicitor draft a will. While some legal knowledge might assist, if you have little property to leave, or the way you want to distribute it is not complex, you can do it yourself on a printed form or go to the Public Trustee. The Public Trustee will usually do the will free of charge but asks a fee to administer the estate.

Unlike divorces, wills are usually not areas of major battle. If you and your partner discuss and make financial decisions together, it is more than likely that you will discuss wills. If you both contribute to the family income, it is important that each of you knows how you will manage without the other's income.

If you are a woman who has never handled the family finances, your partner may think he is protecting you by keeping you in the dark about his plans and leaving everything in the hands of a trustee. We have all heard of women who didn't even know how to sign a cheque after their husbands died. But many lawyers report that 'after a widow goes through a mourning process [she] blooms. They start out doubting their own capabilities but end up being competent and even enjoy handling their own finances.' Janet Holmes à Court took over her husband's vast business interests after his death and was listed in the 1991 'Australia's Rich' list as being the fourth richest person in Australia, with $750 million.[3]

Wills play a slightly different role in second marriages. Many couples, especially if they have children from first marriages, want prenuptial agreements in order to be sure that money will go to their children from a first marriage. If your partner is leaving money in trust, where you get the interest and his children get the principal, conflicts can easily develop. Sometimes, you don't need a second marriage for that to happen. One widow tells of wanting to buy a townhouse on the Gold Coast in which to spend time with her new partner. Her children were enraged that she was spending what they considered their money on another man.

Wills are probably one of the last bastions of tradition, written by lawyers who were raised under old laws and with old attitudes that continue to assume that a woman must be protected by having money doled out to her. Not infrequently, men write wills that give control of family businesses to their sons, while leaving money in trust for their wives and daughters. Often, assets are owned by the husband. He consults a lawyer. The lawyer urges the husband to write a will that protects the money more than it protects the wife. Typically this involves leaving the money in a trust. Unfortunately, this planning sometimes gives you, the widow, the least amount of control over the money.

The message that women are poor managers, despite their better than male records in running small businesses, seems to pervade the legal profession as well as the estate planning contingent. And the best way not to leave money directly to your wife, child or husband, is by leaving money in trust.

TRUSTS

Trusts are devices that place an obligation on a person to deal with property for the benefit of another. Trusts are great in certain situations. If you and your partner die in an accident, you would certainly want money left in trust for your children.

If you have elderly parents, you might want to establish trusts to take care of them, if something happened to you. Trusts are not as advisable if you have few assets. If you and your partner are young, then leaving money *to each other* in trust may not make sense, since management fees would have to be paid year after year.

You can establish a trust while you are alive. This is called an *inter vivos* trust. Trusts that are established by your will are called *testamentary* trusts. Trusts can also be revocable or irrevocable. While you are alive, you might want revocable trusts, in case you change your mind about the trustee.

When you die, your executor is responsible for setting up any testamentary trusts called for by your will. The trust then becomes a separate legal entity that pays taxes. So what should you do? Know as much as possible about your family finances. Discuss your intentions and your partner's. If he can't think about writing a will, make the appointment with the lawyer yourself, then tell him what you've done. He'll probably go with you.

Above all, discuss possible trustees with your partner. Trustees can wield great power.

HOW TRUSTS WORK

A trust is a device that places an obligation on the trustee, as owner of some trust property, to deal with it for the benefit of another person (the beneficiary) or for the advancement of certain purposes.

The trustee can be a person, a commercial or private

company or the Public Trustee. Some trustee companies have been set up by statute, while others are privately incorporated.

High standards of trusteeship are offered by and expected of trustee companies because they hold themselves out as having special skills and experience and are thus entitled to charge fees for acting. Fees are regulated by legislation. Trustees have a right to be reimbursed for any expenses incurred in the administration of the trust.

Each state has a Public Trustee who is empowered to act as executor and trustee of estates. Many people who don't have a friend who is willing to be a trustee approach the Public Trustee. In most states, no more than four trustees may be constituted trustees of a private trust.

The trustee must carry out the obligations set out in the trust agreement, such as managing the assets by investing them, paying out the income, or running a business. Choosing a trustee is crucial if you plan to leave money in trust for your children, your parents or your partner. It's also important if your partner plans to leave money in trust for you. The person who establishes the trust can give the trustee broad or narrow powers. If you give the trustee broad powers, you should be sure the trustee is somebody with good judgement.

CHOOSING a TRUSTEE

How do you choose between appointing a trusted friend and a professional trustee? The professional trustee will usually try to suggest that they will be there long after your trusted friend is gone. The number of commercial companies that have failed over the past few years makes that argument somewhat less forceful than it used to be. Furthermore, when you appoint a company as a trustee, you can never be sure who in the company will actually manage your trust. It could be a recent MBA graduate, learning the ropes on your trust, or it could be a venerable old gentleman who never made it out of the trust department.

When choosing a trustee, keep in mind the possible conflict a trustee has. If you have a trust with $1 million in it and the trustee is paid a 1 per cent fee for managing it, that means the trustee earns $10,000 a year. If you, the wife, would like to withdraw a few hundred thousand dollars out of your trust to buy a new house, the trustee may decide it's not a good idea—one reason being that the trustee's fee will drop if the assets diminish.

Another problem with trusts is that they are supposed to pay out the income. This is all very well if the trusts are invested in investments paying 9 per cent. But if the yield drops to 5 per cent, you would suddenly have a big drop in income. Trusts must allow for this kind of shift and therefore must be flexible in the way they invest, as well as in the way they pay out money. The trustee should understand that the donor of the trust would rather see the trust diminish and have you maintain your standard of living.

A trust agreement that is too rigid could turn out to be a disaster. One man set up a trust where his wife was to receive only the income. The balance was to go to charity when she died. His wife outlived him by thirty years. Inflation totally eroded the buying power of her income and she had to spend her old age living on very little.

An important question is, should you name your partner as a trustee and should he name you? The answer is easy. Name your partner, and ask him to name you, as trustee. It doesn't matter that you may not know how to invest money. If the situation arises, no one will be more concerned about hiring good money managers for your money than you. If you don't know, you will learn. Some women even report that having to deal with money and investments gave them a sense of control that gradually helped them to rebuild their lives.

CHOOSING an EXECUTOR

You and your partner will also have to decide about executors for your wills. The executor's role is slightly different from the trustee's. The basic job of the executor is to carry out the instructions in your will. While this calls for many technical and legal responsibilities, you do not have to name a lawyer or a professional for the job. If you become the executor, you can hire a lawyer to do the work. Executors can be paid fees based on a percentage of the assets of the estate. Lawyers can be hired to do the specific tasks, for a lot less, in some cases.

The executor files the will for probate, pays any debts that are due, pays the funeral expenses, and lists the assets and liabilities. (This is the kind of information you should have, anyway.) As with trustees, you can name a close friend or a professional institution. If you do name a friend, be sure to tell the friend. Being an executor is time consuming and not everyone wants to take on the job. Be careful about naming an institution that may only take an estate of a minimum size.

The best choice of an executor is probably your partner for your will, and you for your partner's will. As you get older, or if the estate is large, you might appoint a younger co-executor.

WHAT YOU SHOULD KNOW ABOUT YOUR PARTNER'S WILL

1 Where is it?

2 If there is a trust, what type of trust? What are its terms?

3 What, if anything, is left for the children?

4 Who are the trustees?

5 Who are the executors?

While these are the things that will be part of the will, there is other information that you should also know.

If your partner runs his own business, will you know what to do to keep it running and will you be able to meet the immediate payroll? Is there someone who can step in to take over? Have you discussed this with your partner?

If you and your partner are in business together, or the business is yours, there are several routes to take. If it's your business or your partner's and you have business partners, you could have a buy–sell agreement. This usually establishes a fixed price at which one of you buys out the other. If your partner has such an agreement, you should know about it. The big problem here is not revaluing the business. You could end up having your partner's share bought out by his business partners at a price that was established years ago, while the business has continued to grow. Or, worse still, you might have to buy out a business partner at an overvalued price that was established when things were going well, but since then the business has collapsed.

You might have a family business that you would like to keep in the family. The usual way of doing this is to give your children shares when the business is just beginning. In this way they become owners at low cost. If the children are very young the shares can be put into trust.

While all of this may seem remote, especially if you are young, it can happen to anyone. Knowing a little about your situation can take away the anxiety and fear that you will be unable to manage.

A GUIDE to BEING ALONE

Technically, if your husband dies, you are a widow. The word comes from the Old English. In addition to its primary meaning as a woman who has lost her husband, the word is defined as 'empty' or 'extra hand at the card table'. Unfortunately, that is also the way many people, even friends, will sometimes regard you once you are no longer part of a couple. Although being alone can be difficult, 'widow' should not become the role definition for your life.

WHAT IF YOU WERE SUDDENLY WIDOWED?

1. How would you meet the monthly expenses that are now paid by your joint incomes? Most couples cover this gap by having life insurance.

2. Would you have enough cash for funeral expenses? Here's where a separate account, which can't be frozen, is helpful.

3. Would you be eligible for Social Security benefits (see Chapter 7)?

4. Would you be able to continue living in your house? Frequently couples have mortgage insurance, which pays off the house if the husband dies. This may not be the best way to insure your house. You should consider having life insurance, for the amount of the mortgage. Coverage might be cheaper. In addition, the insurance would go directly to you, and you could continue the mortgage payments. You would have more control over making a decision about your house than if the mortgage was paid automatically.

5. How would you pay for your children's education? Would you have enough to support them through school and university?

6. What if you have a lot of debts?

IMMEDIATE STEPS TO TAKE

Plan the funeral. While you might feel that it is important to arrange a more lavish service than you can really afford, it is probably not the best use of your money, especially if you are uncertain of your future finances. Your local funeral director will be able to tell you the proper procedures. But remember, you can have whatever touches you would like.

Costs average around $3000–$4000. Much depends on the elaborateness of the casket you choose and the number of cars you have for the cemetery.

You may also want to place a notice in your local newspaper. The clergyman is generally paid a small amount in cash.

Some people plan funerals in advance. There are even prepaid plans. You can check prices at a few funeral homes before making a decision. You can even have a trust where your money will accumulate, until needed, and earn interest. You also have to be sure that inflation is figured into your plan so that there will be no extra charges.

DURING THE FIRST MONTH

Find the will. Most wills have to be probated—that is, they have to be proved as valid. Generally when the estate is very small, under about $15,000, there is no need to obtain probate. The need for probate also depends on the amount of the estate, how the money is held, and certainty about the existence and operation of the will. While an individual can go through the probate process alone, you are probably better off hiring a lawyer. Probate does not have to be done immediately, but within the first few weeks is advisable.

IN THE FIRST THREE MONTHS

You will need copies of the death certificate; in some cases these must be certified. The funeral director can help you with this. You need the certificate in order to collect life insurance and anything else for which you may be the beneficiary.

TRANSFER THE FOLLOWING TO YOUR NAME:
◆ *Title to your house, if it was jointly owned.*

◆ Bank accounts. Joint accounts could be frozen, which is one reason you should have an account in your own name.

◆ Credit cards. If you have credit cards in your own name, you can continue to use them. If your credit cards are all in your partner's name, and you signed on them, you can probably continue to use them. As long as you continue to pay on time, you will not have any problems. However, you will probably at some time want to notify the company and have the cards changed to your name. Be sure you have records to document that you were an authorised signatory. If you had a joint credit card, notify the company that the card should be in your name only.

◆ Securities. Call the broker.

LIFE INSURANCE

Notify the insurance company, either directly or through your insurance agent. The named beneficiary is paid directly, usually in two to three weeks. You will need a death certificate. If your partner had group life insurance through his employer, you should contact the employer about collecting. Be prepared to be robust. Remember my friend whose mother was challenged by the insurance company when a claim was made following her husband's death? The company claimed his insurance was void because of a pre-existing illness that had not been declared. A medical certificate from the doctor did the trick, but it was a harrowing time before the insurance company came around.

MORTGAGE INSURANCE

If you have mortgage insurance, it was probably arranged through your bank and you should contact the bank about this.

SUPERANNUATION

Contact the employer to find out about any payouts that may be due to you.

INVESTMENTS

If you are unfamiliar with your partner's investments, call the broker and have the statements sent to you. Then ask the broker to explain why the various stocks and bonds were chosen.

DEBTS

If debts were in your partner's name only, his estate must pay them; if they were in your joint names, you may have to pay them. Check the status of:

◆ *outstanding loans.*

◆ *car payments.*

◆ *credit card payments—if the card is only in your partner's name, cancel it. Your partner's estate is responsible for any outstanding credit card payments.*

TAXES

You will have to file an income tax return as usual.

YOUR WILL

If your partner was the executor of your will, you will need to name someone else. If your partner was the beneficiary of your life insurance, change this.

GO BACK TO WORK

If you were working, go back to work, not only for the income, but because having something to do each day will help.

TAKE A LOOK AT YOUR FINANCES

◆ *Redo your asset and liability statement.*

◆ *Redo your income and outgoings statement.*

◆ *Review your insurance. If you have young children, you may need life insurance. If you are working, you may need disability insurance.*

WHAT NOT TO DO

1. Don't make any decisions about selling your house, unless this is something you had carefully planned before.
2. Don't buy anything from anybody—especially if the seller claims it will give you an income for life.

OTHER THINGS TO DO

INVESTMENTS
If your partner always invested your money, and you suddenly find that you have received the proceeds from his life insurance in a lump sum, immediately put the money into a bank, or treasury bonds, or a money market fund offered by one of the larger mutual fund companies. Don't even think about doing anything else, no matter who recommends it. It's your money now. You will have time to decide how to invest it.

YOUR HOUSE
Think about whether you want to keep your house. This should not just be based on economics, but on your feelings as well. The finances are easy to calculate. If your income is now considerably less, you will have to decide whether you are making a sacrifice out of some loyalty to the marital home, or to your children who don't want you to sell. Don't be pushed into selling quickly by an aggressive—or an overly-sympathetic—estate agent.

SPECIAL ADVICE
for OLDER WOMEN

You want to be sure that you will be taken care of in your old age. Many of my friends have parents who are now getting old.

The situation is often the same: everything is fine until the father dies and the mother is alone. The mother is fine for the first few years. Then she may begin to fail—sometimes it's her health, sometimes her mind.

One friend's mother, living alone in a Gold Coast condominium, began to imagine that people were trying to break into her apartment. My friend and her two sisters pooled their money and bought a small house in which one sister lived with the mother. This worked for a while, but eventually the mother needed the care of a nursing home. If you have children, discuss with them the possibilities of what might happen to you and how you would like things handled.

Here are a few things to consider:

◆ *The possibility of buying into a retirement community.*

◆ *Selling your house while you still have the energy to move and the house has not become a burden.*

◆ *If you do not have children, or feel that they are too far away to be of help should you have problems, find someone experienced with whom you can discuss your future.*

◆ *You may want to consider giving away some of your assets in order to qualify for nursing home care.*

◆ *If you are managing your own assets, you may want to put them in a living trust to make it easier for someone else to take over.*

FIVE COMMON MISTAKES OF WOMEN WHOSE PARTNERS ALWAYS DID EVERYTHING FOR THEM

Many women who are alone and faced for the first time with having to handle their own money make the following mistakes:

1. They think if their partners did it a particular way, it must be right. An example is the woman who inherited savings that had been yielding 9 per cent. When interest dropped, she refused to do anything else with the money.

2. They are unwilling to take investment risks. By not taking any risk, their investments don't keep pace with inflation and they keep having to reduce their expenses because their dollars buy less and less. Your money has to generate increasing, not diminishing, income. This is easy advice to give, because it is logical. But, in the end, you have to be able to feel comfortable with it. If thinking about what you perceive as a risk is going to keep you awake at night, don't do it.

3. They give loans to their children. This leaves them with even less money, which makes them even more fearful and unable to manage. Often women, left alone after long marriages, feel life is not going to offer much any more, or they feel guilty for surviving. They are therefore vulnerable to requests from their children, who frequently promise to pay them back but often have problems that make this impossible. Resist the temptation.

4. They meet a new man and let him take charge, because they feel they can't handle money. Most women can, and should, handle their own investments—if not on a daily basis, at least frequently consulting a broker or adviser.

5. They are unable to understand the reality of their new situations and so fail to reduce their expenses. An example of what can happen is a couple where the husband's income had been $75,000. The wife didn't work. After her husband died, she was left with assets of $250,000. Her income dropped to below $25,000. This was a drastic change, which she couldn't accept.

Because women generally live longer than men, many will face a period on their own, without the support of a partner. The more knowledge you have beforehand, the better equipped you will be. But even if you are starting out with little awareness, you can learn quickly. One woman, who had always taken charge of everything, said she learned the most by asking her friends. She never asked for general advice, but always for specific information. If a friend knew about cars, she asked that friend. If another friend knew about insurance, she would ask that friend her insurance questions. You may not have such competent friends, but you can do a lot of your own research, and you can learn.

CINDERELLA REVISED: the RIGHTS of CHILDREN

It's true, there are never any evil stepfathers. Only a bunch of lily-livered widowers who let me get away with murder vis-à-vis their daughters. Where are they when I'm making those girls drudge in the kitchen, or sending them out into the blizzard in their paper dresses? Working late at the office. Passing the buck. Men! But if you think they knew nothing about it, you're crazy.

– MARGARET ATTWOOD, *GOOD BONES*

FOLK TALES HAVE IT THAT wicked stepmothers (and lily-livered widowers) rode roughshod over their children. Not any more. Children's rights have changed dramatically over the centuries. In ancient Rome, children were raised at the whim of the father. When the child was born, the father could either keep it or order it left exposed. When a baby was born, the midwife placed the child on the ground. The father could either lift up the child, signifying his intention of raising the child, or leave it on the ground to die. Often children were left to die in order to preserve the inheritance of the children already living. They were also frequently given up for adoption, particularly when the natural parents could not afford to give the child advantages. Octavius, who became the emperor Augustus, was the adopted son of Julius Caesar. Children were used in order to form political alliances, make advantageous marriages or serve in other ways the aims of their parents.[1]

Roman sons remained subject to their father's rule until the father died. (Roman women were under the thumb first of their father and then their husband.) The earnings of the son also belonged to the father. Fathers could disinherit their sons. And, since Roman women often died in childbirth, a stepmother, who could influence the father, could prove to be a great threat to the children of a first marriage.

Australians have moved a long way from pagan Rome. The rights of children are increasingly protected by national and international laws.

LAWS PROTECTING CHILDREN

The official definition of child is a person who has not reached the age of majority, usually eighteen. Australian children have specific rights. They are, at least theoretically, protected from the abuse of parents—and in Victoria have even 'divorced' their parents. A court order can remove children from a home where abuse is suspected. After children turn eighteen and are legally adults, they are no longer the responsibility of their parents.

Our legal heritage derives from England, where in the 19th century mothers had no rights over their children. It should be part of our cultural heritage to repeat the story of Lady Caroline Norton to our daughters.

In 1836 George Norton, a London lawyer and former Tory MP, brought a suit against the Prime Minister for seducing his wife, Lady Caroline—granddaughter of R. B. Sheridan, the playwright. She was bright and beautiful—an author, musician and poet who had been raised in the upper echelons of London society.

Lady Caroline's husband's accusations were disproved, but her reputation was nonetheless tarnished. She left her husband (divorce was not available) and fought a bitter custody battle over their children whom George Norton, as legal guardian, had removed from their mother. He refused to let her see or contact them.

At that time under common law, the children of a marriage 'belonged' to the father; the mother had no rights at all. Indeed, as Lady Caroline stated in words that reflect those of women today who claim coercion by their husbands over property settlements:

But the question is on what principle the legislature should give a man this power to torment; this power to say to his wife 'You shall bear blows, you shall bear inconstancy, you shall give up property, you shall endure insult, and yet you shall continue to live under my roof, or else I will take your children and you will never see them more'? [2]

In response to the pleas of Lady Caroline and others, the Infant Custody Bill was passed and became law in 1839. Over the next 150 years, women's rights to their children and the belief that they were the appropriate people to raise small children became embedded in our culture. By the 20th century there was a complete about-turn from earlier times, with mothers, until recently, almost always being awarded custody of their children unless there was an extremely unusual circumstance. Fathers paid support—or at least were supposed to.

In the last few decades, however, fathers, claiming equal rights, have begun to seek custody of their children.

The increasing number of step-parents and blended families has further complicated the idea of child custody, throwing doubt on to the once sacred doctrine that the natural parents should raise children. One example is the child who was raised by a mother and stepfather. In the past, if the mother died, the natural father would automatically be given custody of the child, even if he had previously abandoned that child.

Today, the best interests of the child are the primary consideration of the courts in determining custody, and custody might be awarded to the stepfather who had raised the child. And in a materialistic society such as ours, it may well happen that courts start to see the best interests of the child associated with the parent who can provide them with greater material advantages, a factor that does not bode well for women, who almost always earn less than their ex-partners.

Children have the right to make contracts with adults and to have these contracts enforced. On the other hand, children cannot have contracts with adults enforced against them.

Parents also have certain obligations toward their children. Children are entitled to support and education. They also have the right to medical care. Sometimes this right is enforced by courts when the religious beliefs of parents may prohibit medical intervention.

The money that children earn or inherit is also protected. An example might be a child actress who earns a high salary. Her salary must be used only for her support. In one situation, the mother of a young actress became ill and had no health insurance. The mother, who had guided her daughter's career, could not use any of her daughter's money for medical expenses, even though the daughter would have wanted to help her mother. Parents must consider themselves guardians of the money. Occasionally, children have sued parents and accused them of mismanaging funds left for them. It is not at all unusual for children to challenge the wills of their parents if they feel they have been unfairly disinherited.

A family in Melbourne received an unhappy shock following the death of the husband and father. The father had been very religious; the three daughters were agnostic, single and feminist. After his death it was discovered he had left his entire estate to the church, with his relatively young wife permitted to reside in the matrimonial home until her death, when it too reverted to the church. After much angst and some rage, legal advice was sought. Negotiations were initially unsuccessful with the church. It was only after formal proceedings had been commenced, and with the assistance of legislation similar to the Family Provisions Act, that the surviving family were able to overturn the harsh provisions of the will.

Children who are born outside of marriage (legally referred to as 'ex-nuptial children') have equal rights with children born within the marriage to inherit from their parents—whether or not the parents made wills. This came about under specific legislation that abolished the idea of 'illegitimate' children. It was at last recognised that 'illegitimacy' was very much a patriarchal notion, reflecting the father's interest in and control over offspring. No mother, having given birth, is likely to label her new-born child as illegitimate! It is quite obviously and legitimately hers, regardless of her current relationship with the father.

At the same time that illegitimacy was removed from the law, fathers of ex-nuptial children were recognised as their joint legal guardians. This works well for the state, which wants men to pay for the costs of bringing up their children. However, it is a problem for women who decide to have a child on their own.

DIVORCE and the CHILDREN

Should you divorce, the law becomes quite specific about your obligations to your children. Children of a marriage or de facto relationship and children whose parents have no continuing relationship are all covered by the same provisions of the *Family Law Act*. As recently retired Family Court judge Justice Nygh has stated, 'The law is moving to a position where legal consequences are attached to cohabitation rather than marriage. For example, the liability to support a child arises out of the fact that you have a child, not that you are married... Taken to a logical consequence, you would arrive at a position where one no longer enquires whether the parties are married, but whether they live together.'[3]

Child support and child custody are carefully spelled out in divorce and separation agreements. However, during marriage, parents must make their own rules about how to raise their children.

For many couples, the decision to have children is the most important decision they will make. For many women, the decision may be even more critical than for men, because the birth of a child often changes their position as equals in the relationship. It certainly changes their work patterns. No matter how equally a couple may decide to divide marital obligations, it is still the mother who must physically give birth to the child. The mother is also most often the person who remains responsible for that child. More often than not, it is the mother who cuts back on her career, forfeits some of her earlier goals, in order to take care of her child. And, should the relationship end in divorce, mothers, not fathers, end up with custody and responsibility for four out of every five children.

One woman reports, 'As soon as our daughter was born, my husband saw me as a mother. He expected me to do things his mother had done, including staying home with our child.' Women frequently discover that their partners no longer want them to be wage-earning equals. Many women feel pushed into a dependent role, and, as already discussed, discover that instead of mutually agreed upon financial decisions, partners now assume a controlling role in the decision making. Should you divorce, child support and child custody can loom as major areas of conflict.

THE CHILD SUPPORT AGENCY

Until 1989 when the Child Support Scheme was introduced to Australia, up to 80 per cent of separated partners were not paying child support. This meant that custodial parents— almost exclusively women—were increasingly relying on Social Security payments. Now if payments are not made, the custodial parent can apply for support from the Child Support Agency.

The Child Support Agency is part of the tax office. When parents do not come to a satisfactory agreement about child support, the Agency applies a formula and determines the amount that should be paid. The formula, which is based on taxable income, allows for deductions of both the custodial and non-custodial parent and any other dependent children they now have. The Agency manages the collection of the money, either by arranging for an employer to deduct if from the parent's pay or by having the parent pay it directly to the Agency. In recently announced changes to the scheme, it will in future be possible to receive payments directly from ex-partners.

When fathers deny paternity, the Family Court has the power to order blood tests to assist in proving a connection between father and child. If parentage is proved, the Child Support Agency will accept an application for child support from the custodial parent.

When Diana and Robert divorced, Robert agreed to pay $45 a week for each child as maintenance. He continued to pay this amount fairly regularly (although Diana often had to ask for it—a situation which she thought he enjoyed) for three years until the children were nine and five. At that time, however, Robert and his new wife started a family and he claimed that he could no longer afford the $90 a week. He informed Diana, in writing, that he would henceforth pay only $50 a week for the two children of the first marriage.

Diana applied to the Child Support Agency. Taking into account Robert's salary and financial obligations to his new family and Diana's part-time income, an assessment of $30 a week for each child was made.

One problem with child support awards is the non-monetary costs that are usually borne by the mother. Studies estimate that divorced mothers spend between 19.6 and 26.6 hours each week taking care of their children. If a monetary value is put on that time, even paying as little as $15 an hour, the annual cost works out at $19,500 a year!

So much for the theory. In practice, fathers frequently under report income when awards are made and then fail to pay the necessary support after the divorce. On the other hand, there are fathers who go the other way, using their time with the children to lavish material goods on them. Often, when parents divorce, mothers find that they must struggle on a limited budget all week. Then, when the children visit their more affluent father on weekends, he buys them toys and clothes the mother cannot afford. One example was a father who stopped paying support to the children's mother, then entertained the children at a hotel on weekends, allowing them to run up large room-service charges.

In another case, a mother supported her children through university on a limited budget and with no support from the father, who instead gave the children $500 on their birthdays and at Christmas. They thought him generous and kind. She felt less kindly towards him and faced the dilemma of 'protecting' him by keeping quiet or of pointing out to the children that his actions were deliberately aimed at punishing her.

Many women who accept a settlement on divorce because it frees them from a troubled relationship with their ex-husband soon learn that divorce does not stop the troubles when there are children and child support payments involved. A friend who has been divorced now for ten years laments that she gave up all claims to her husband's superannuation 'just to get him out of my hair', only to find that she still has to deal with him regularly over payments for the children.

Sometimes, such arguments are a way of getting back at you. Sometimes, it merely reflects something you knew for a long time while you were married—that your husband liked to control spending. This can lead to scores of petty arguments with a former partner. Sometimes, you may assume an interpretation of support that may be different from your husband's. Don't assume anything.

> When Mary and her husband Jim divorced, their agreement said he would take care of medical expenses not covered by Medicare. Although he could have perfectly well afforded it, Jim refused to pay dental expenses. Mary had assumed that medical and dental were one and the same. She could not have imagined that he would be reluctant to pay for the braces necessary for their two daughters but which the divorce agreement did not specify. Jim was using his money to control the situation, just as he had done during their marriage.

If you expect the children's father to help pay for their education, be sure to specify this in your divorce agreement. Do you mean school only, or university as well? Will he pay for books, uniforms and excursions, or only fees?

Fathers who do not pay child support often are supporting another family. This requires them to manage payments to both lots of children. Not even Solomon would be able to solve some of the complicated financial problems of the modern blended family, although the Child Support Agency with its established formula for deciding custody payments attempts to do so.

DO YOU WANT YOUR CHILDREN to be RICH?

While child support payments are regulated by the law, inheritance is left to the largesse of the parents. In Australia it is not illegal to disinherit one's children although, as discussed, in most states children can challenge the will if they have not been adequately provided for.

If you decide you do not want to leave money to your children, specify this in a will. Without a will, the intestate laws of your state will provide for your children. This usually means that children will inherit between one-third and a half of your estate (see Chapter 8). Should your children inherit money when they are under eighteen years of age, that money will be put into a trust.

Statistically the chances are that you will outlive your partner, and thus be able to provide for your children. But what if you die first? Here is where property ownership can become extremely important. If, for example, you own your home as joint tenants, you cannot leave your share of the house to the children, as it automatically goes to your partner. If you own your property as tenants in common, you can each leave your share to anyone you wish to specify. In other words, you could leave your half to your children, in trust if they are minors.

Australians are living longer and spending much of their money on their own retirement and medical care. They also spend a great deal of money on their children's education. Many also help their married children to buy a house. So, often there is not much money left to leave to children. But as your assets increase, it's a good idea to talk with your partner about exactly what you would like to do for your children.

If you remarry and each of you has children from a first marriage, you may discover that you have very different attitudes towards money, which could cause problems. This is where a prenuptial agreement could be helpful. In the agreement you can arrange to provide for your children in any way that suits you.

You may think that children should have a regular allowance, regardless of whether the money is earned by the performance of household tasks, while your partner may consider an allowance as something that a child must earn. You may want to scrimp and save to send your children to a private school, while your partner may think a state school, like the one he attended, is good enough.

You may discover that you have different ideas about money. Some people are of the 'I did it myself' school, believing that very little money should be left to their children. Others believe that children will benefit from the security of knowing that they will come into some money.

Money left for a child by a parent can also be interpreted by the child as a token of the parent's love. Not leaving money can send a message that the parent may not have intended.

While you probably don't want to see your children left with nothing, it's important to balance your own needs with what you would like to leave them. You should also resist using your property to play power games with your offspring. Tempting as it may be to reward the children who have been good to you and to punish those who have neglected you, this can create enormous difficulties for children if they are left very unequal portions of your estate. Nothing embitters siblings more than to find that the brother who has been careless with money receives a greater share because his (extravagant) needs are seen as greater than those of a sister who has been prudent. Even more galling are the parents who leave more to their son because the daughter has a partner to look after her!

Unlike the French, who divide property equally among their children, the English adopted primogeniture, leaving all the property to the first-born son. Primogeniture is no longer practised as a matter of law, but there are undoubtedly traces of that old tradition still with us. Especially where a son has followed in his father's footsteps into a business or a farm, there is strong pressure to ensure that the son keeps control of that asset, regardless of what this means for the other children. If this is not what you want for your children, you should discuss it—perhaps with them—but certainly with your partner.

If you decide to leave money for your children, you also have to decide how old they should be when they get the money. Lawyers have a tendency to suggest that money be left in trust for a long time. A good solution is to leave the money so that it is gradually given to your children, say one-half at age thirty, and the balance at age forty. Leaving money outright to children could pose a problem, should the children divorce. If you know that you will leave money to a son or daughter, you might discuss with your children the way in which they would like the money left. You might introduce them to the idea of prenuptial agreements, so that they can keep their inherited money separate.

When leaving money for your children, there is also the question of trustees to consider. You need to choose someone who is likely to outlive you and be able to manage that money for a long time. Naming one child as trustee for another child is rarely the best solution.

It suits many men to think that women are not capable of handling money, just as it suits them—in spite of the evidence—to consider that women are poor drivers. This can be very disturbing for mothers who rejoice in their daughters' competence and want to see them taking an equal role with their brothers. It may be up to you to take an active role in promoting that equality.

When there are family businesses, fathers frequently think of bringing in their sons, but only bring in daughters as a last resort. They leave wills that put money in trust for their daughters, while leaving money outright to their sons. Many fathers still do not think of making daughters executors of their estates. Even a much younger, must less stable son is still seen by many fathers as the appropriate person to handle the estate. My own father, well-trained with two feminist daughters, automatically thought of his son as executor of his estate even though one of the daughters was a lawyer.

If you can see that a daughter is a better person to handle the estate, insist that you be heard and that the decision is made on a rational basis—not just because it is an unconsidered 'tradition'. You owe it to her to have a reflected image of herself as a competent and trusted money manager.

TEN

A SENSE of ENTITLEMENT

WHILE THIS BOOK advocates that women should know about money—their own and their partner's—it is advocating something else as well. It urges women to see themselves as the best and most capable person to handle their own finances. It asks them to develop a *sense of entitlement* to the money they have earned and to use it in ways they have purposefully chosen.

In a story that probably doesn't have to be told because we all know the plot, Sally is young, successful and a financial adviser with one of the large banking corporations. She has a law/commerce degree from a good university and spends her days advising people on how to manage their money wisely. She has her own unit, which is almost paid off, a car and enough money to live comfortably and help pay her mother's expenses in a retirement unit. And a boyfriend. He is also young, charming and apparently successful. But he has had some financial problems and Sally has lent him money. At first it was just a loan to tide him over until a new 'deal' came through. He paid it back. Then another loan, a bigger one. And then he asked Sally if she could raise $20,000 for him—just for a few weeks. Against her better judgement, Sally did so. Then she found out that his deals were gambling deals. In spite of all her knowledge and understanding of wise money management, Sally lent money to her partner with no real knowledge of what it was for or where it was going. Now she is faced with losing him—and the $20,000—or hanging in there for her money but with no respect for him—and not much for herself.

Like many of us, Sally found it hard to say no. She had enough money. And he was her partner. In her better moments she rationalises that it was reasonable for her to lend him money. At other times she knows that it was stupid and completely contrary to the advice that she regularly gives to her clients.

Many of us accept without thinking that we are not really entitled to money—even the money we have earned ourselves. We have an awful tendency to give things away—even when doing so means some hardship for ourselves. It's a bit like the burnt toast syndrome. My mother got so used to eating the burnt-toast that she started to like burnt toast. Or the family roast. The best and biggest parts of the leg of lamb go to the boys, never to the girls or to the cook who has slaved over the hot oven.

Saying no when demands are made on us, particularly financial demands, is often regarded as selfishness. After all, what needs do we have that aren't being met? Why shouldn't we give any 'extra' money to the children, or to our partners?

But there are two kinds of 'selfishness'. One is the negative kind that is demonstrated when people look after themselves at other people's expense. The other is a positive kind. It is a 'self'ishness that allows an individual to realistically assess their own worth, to know their needs and to meet them, without apology. It allows people to have a sense of agency in dealing with the world.

The alternative, even for women like Sally who 'know' about handling money, is to become the 'self'-less person who, in meeting other people's needs first, can end up being seen as having no real needs of her own. And it is easy to take on that image of ourselves.

As women, we have a long tradition of folk tales, urban myths and a selectively recorded history that portrays the ideal woman as compliant, selfless and devoted to her family. Such an ideal conveniently encourages us to hand over our money and our independence because it makes other people feel better and stronger.

Virginia Woolf once stated that women have for centuries acted as looking glasses for men, reflecting them at twice their natural size. We are in danger of being the opposite: of being reflected at half our natural size—with only half of our needs acknowledged and met. We should actively resist that tradition and create a new one. We should, at each stage of our lives, be developing a realistic sense of self. Most of us will be alone at some stage—and need it.

Take the situation faced by the 1991 Bulletin/Qantas Businesswoman of the Year, Sara Henderson, She and her husband, who was described as 'hopelessly innumerate and profligate, abysmally self-centred and endlessly priapic',[1] owned Bullo River Station in the Northern Territory, a property 'the size of metropolitan Sydney'. When her husband died in 1986, Sara inherited debts of half a million dollars, and had three daughters to support.

In less than a decade, she managed to turn round the financial disaster and become Businesswoman of the Year. She upgraded the herd on Bullo River, opened tourist facilities on the property and made money from putting the property's heavy machinery to work in a contracting venture. She wrote a best-selling book and has become one of the most sought-after speakers on the lecture circuit.

It is of no value simply to understand theoretically what you can and should know and do. Like Sara Henderson, you must have the motivation to act. It doesn't matter whether it is born of anger, frustration or a sheer determination to succeed. It doesn't even matter if for a while you 'act out' the role as agent in your own life. When you start to act, you are seen as a force to be reckoned with: doors open and plans are realised.

If this means insisting on keeping your own money or on having a prenuptial agreement, even though your partner doesn't like it, stand firm. If it means making him wait for you to sign a loan document until you have had separate financial advice, make him wait. If it means refusing to sign company documents as a director unless you are allowed to play an active role as a director, then refuse firmly and politely. Point out that you are being reasonable and responsible, that signing has legal consequences that you take seriously. In the long run, people will think better of you for taking your role seriously. And it may save you from debts, or even a stint in gaol.

If you are one of the 35-plus per cent of married women who has to deal with divorce and a property settlement, don't be talked into thinking that your contributions to the marriage were less because they were not paid for in dollars. Don't be good-natured and generous when the superannuation is discussed. For every dollar that is due, half of it should be yours. If it hadn't been for you fulfilling your part of the partnership, he could not have done his and neither of you would have access to the superannuation. If there seems to be no resolution, suggest that the superannuation be split into two policies, with each of you taking half of the accrued benefits.

Don't think of it as being cynical and unfeminine to want to know about the family finances. To be familiar with information is to be able to act competently and confidently if a crisis arises. If this upsets those around you who would prefer you to be dependent and compliant that is their problem, not yours.

And finally, think of yourself as a role model. It's not good enough to capitulate and at the same time hope that your daughters will somehow learn to be different and not make the same mistakes as you. Let them see you avoiding the mistakes in the first place. The best way for them to learn a sense of entitlement and to appreciate their own worth is for you to demonstrate it in your life. One of the most valuable things you can give your daughters—and your sons—is the model of a wise woman who, in matters of money and management, is her own person.

ENDNOTES

CHAPTER 1

1. Jocelynne Scutt, *Women and the Law*, The Law Book Co., 1990, p. 30.

2. Hugh Mackay, *Reinventing Australia*, Angus & Robertson, Sydney, 1993, p. 25.

3. Ibid., p. 35.

4. Michael Bittman (ed.), *Juggling Time: How Australian Families Use Time*, Office of the Status of Women, 1991, p. 9.

5. Ibid., p. 7.

6. Beth Ann Shelton, 'The Distribution of Household Tasks, Does a Wife's Employment Make a Difference', *Journal of Family Issues*, Vol. 11, June 1990, pp. 131–132.

7. Michael Bittman (ed.), *Juggling Time: How Australian Families Use Time*, Office of the Status of Women, 1991, p. 17.

8. *Life Matters with Geraldine Doogue*, A.B.C. Radio National program, 30 March 1994.

9. Jessie Bernard, *The Future of Marriage*, World Publishing, New York, 1972, p. 41.

10. *Working Woman*, January 1992, p. 53.

11. *Savvy*, February 1990.

12. '*But I Wouldn't Want My Wife To Work Here*': A Study of Migrant Women in Melbourne Industry, Centre for Urban Research and Action, Melbourne, 1976.

13. Tamar Lewin, 'For some two-paycheck families, the economics don't add up,' *New York Times*, 21 April 1991; Elizabeth Ritchies Johnson, 'I Couldn't Afford My Job', Redbook, April 1991, p. 89.

14. Peter McDonald (ed.), *Settling Up—Property and Income Distribution on Divorce in Australia*, Australian Institute of Family Studies, 1986, p. 42.

15. Lynn K. White and Tang Shengming, *The Economic Foundations of Marital Happiness and Divorce*, unpublished, 1992.

16. Virginia Dowd, quoted in 'Balancing Act', *HQ*, Spring 1992, p. 140.

17. Survey, Oppenheimer Management Corporation, unpublished, March 1992.

CHAPTER 2

1. M. J. Gage, *Woman, Church & State*, Persephone Press, Massachusetts, 1980, p. 52.

2. *Blackstone's Commentaries*, Vol. 1, p. 442.

3. Charles Dickens, *Oliver Twist*, Ch. 51.

4. Albie Sachs and Joan Hoff Wilson, *Sexism and the Law*, Martin Robertson, 1978, p. 136.

5. Carol Bauer and Lawrence Ritt, *Free & Ennobled*, Pergamon Press, Oxford, 1979, p. 29.

6. 'Don't be a Money Moron', *SHE*, April 1994, p. 61.

7. 'Balancing Act', *HQ*, Spring 1992, p. 141.

8. 'Don't be a Money Moron', *SHE*, April 1994, p. 61.

9. Private conversation, 1993.

CHAPTER 3

1. Margaret Harrison, *Australian Family Briefings No. 2*, Australian Institute of Family Studies, February 1993.

2. *The Wall Street Journal*, 29 October 1991.

3. Bureau of Labour Statistics, *Consumer Expenditures in 1990*.

CHAPTER 4

1. T. Roth, *Babylonian Marriage Agreements, Seventh to the Third Centuries B.C.*, Verlag, Butzon and Becker Kevelaer, Germany, 1989.

2. Lady Anne Somerset, 'Elizabeth I', *Connoisseur*, November 1991, pp. 140–142.

3. Lisa Green, 'Bound by Law', *Elle*, April 1994, p. 62.

4. Joann S. Lublin, 'Lone Star report says ex-chief charged firm $1.1 million for personal expenses', *The Wall Street Journal*, 3 May 1991.

5. *Neilson v Neilson*, 780 Pacific 2d 1264 Utah, 1989, *Family Law Quarterly*, Vol. xxiv, No. 4, Winter 1991, p. 392.

6. Appendix, 'Uniform Premarital Agreement Act', *Baylor Law Review*, Vol. 42, 1990, p. 830.

7. *D'Amato v D'Amato*, Florida, 176, Southern 2d, pp. 907–909.

8. *Lutgert v Lutgert*, 338 Southern 2d 1111.

9. Maureen Orth, 'What's Love Got to Do With It?', *Vanity Fair*, August 1990, p. 128.

10. Lisa Green, 'Bound by Law', *Elle*, April 1994, p. 64.

11. Ibid., p. 66.

12. 'Post-divorce doubts can't undo a prenuptial agreement, judge rules in Bingham case', *New York Times*, 1 January 1992.

13. *McKee-Johnson v Johnson*, 444 North Western 2d 259, Minnesota, 1989, *Family Law Quarterly*, Vol. xxiv, No. 4, Winter 1991, p. 391.

14. *Gross v Gross*, 11 Ohio St 3rd 99, 464 NE 2d 500 (1984).

CHAPTER 5

1. *Soblusky & Soblusky* (1976) FLC 90-124.

2. *Barkley & Barkley* (1976) FLC 90-126.

3. *Evans & Evans* (1790) 1 Hag Con 35 at 36, in H. A. Finlay, *Family Law in Australia*, 2nd edn, Butterworths, Sydney, 1978.

4. Annamay T. Sheppard, 'Women, Families & Equality: Was Divorce Reform a Mistake?', in *Women's Rights Law Reporter*, Vol. 12, No. 3, Fall 1990, p. 144.

5. Jocelynne Scutt, *Women and the Law*, The Law Book Co., Sydney, 1990, p. 212.

6. Private conversation, April 1994.

7. *Currie & Currie* (1976) FLC 90-101.

8. *Australian Women and Economic Security,* Social Welfare Research Centre, University of New South Wales, Sydney, 1988.

9. Peter McDonald (ed.), *Settling Up—Property and Income Distribution on Divorce in Australia,* Australian Institute of Family Studies, 1986, p. 260.

CHAPTER 6

1. Jocelynne Scutt, *Women and the Law,* The Law Book Co., Sydney, 1990, p. 207.

2. Ibid., p. 212.

3. Lynn Hecht Schafran, 'Gender Bias in the Courts: An Emerging Focus for Judicial Reform', *Arizona State Law Journal,* Vol. 21, 1989, p. 240.

4. Peter McDonald (ed.), *Settling Up—Property and Income Distribution on Divorce in Australia,* Australian Institute of Family Studies, 1986, Ch. 11.

5. Ibid., p. 222.

6. Ibid.

7. Ibid.

8. *Sydney Morning Herald,* 24 March 1994.

9. Ibid.

10. Peter McDonald (ed.), *Settling Up—Property and Income Distribution on Divorce in Australia,* Australian Institute of Family Studies, 1986, p. 221.

11. Ibid.

12. Ibid., p. 220.

13. Private conversation.

14. Private conversation, 27 April 1994.

15. Michael Lavarch, Federal Attorney General, quoted in *Sydney Morning Herald,* 17 December 1993.

CHAPTER 7

1. Fritz Stern, *Gold and Iron*, Alfred A. Knopf, New York, 1977, pp. 208–209.

2. *Women in Australia*, Australian Bureau of Statistics, Catalogue No. 4113.0, 1993.

3. Ibid.

4. Hugh Mackay, *The Weekend Review*, 26–27 March 1994.

5. Neil Chenoweth, 'Work your way to poverty', *The Bulletin*, 27 July 1993.

6. Private conversation, March 1994.

7. *Sydney Morning Herald*, 24 March 1994.

8. *The Law Handbook*, 4th edn, Redfern Legal Publishing 1991, Sydney, Lynne Spender (ed.), 1991, p. 440.

9. Linda Roseman, Arthur Shulman and Michelle Levine, *Widowed Families with Children: Personal need and societal response*, Working Paper No. 7, May 1984, p. 15.

10. Catherine Armitage, 'After the divorce, who gets the super?', *Sydney Morning Herald*, 12 January 1994.

11. Ibid.

12. Adapted from Bob Rosefsky, *Money Talks*, McGraw-Hill Publishing Company, New York, 1989, p. 535.

13. *Women in Australia*, Australian Bureau of Statistics, Catalogue No. 4113.0, 1993.

CHAPTER 8

1. Nathan Ross, MD, *The Psychiatry of Writing a Will,* Charles C. Thomas, Springfield, Illinois, 1989, pp. 52–53.

2. Luncheon for Mrs Vincent Astor, sponsored by the World Monuments Association, 22 October 1991.

3. *Australian Business Monthly*, September 1991.

CHAPTER 9

1. P. Aries and G. Duby (eds), *A History of Private Lives from Pagan Rome to Byzantium,* The Belknap Press of Harvard University Press, Cambridge, Massachusetts, 1987, pp. 9–11.

2. Carol Bauer and Lawrence Ritt, 'A Plain Letter to the Lord Chancellor on the Infant Custody Bill', written by Caroline Norton as Pearce Stevenson, in *Free & Ennobled,* Pergamon Press, Oxford, 1979, p. 181.

3. Jane Fraser, 'The woman from Bullo River', *The Australian Magazine,* 23–24 April 1994, pp. 8–13.

CHAPTER 10

1. Jane Fraser, 'The woman from Bullo River', *The Australian Magazine,* 23–24 April 1994. pp. 8–13.

SELECT BIBLIOGRAPHY

Aries, Philippe and George Duby (eds), *A History of Private Life: From Pagan Rome to Byzantium*, The Belknap Press of Harvard University Press, Cambridge, Massachusetts, 1987.

Australian Bureau of Statistics, *Women in Australia*, Catalogue No. 4113.0, 1993.

Bauer, Carol and Lawrence Ritt, *Free & Ennobled*, Pergamon Press, Oxford, 1979.

Bernard, Jessie, *The Future of Marriage*, World Publishing, New York, 1972.

Bittman, Michael and Australian Bureau of Statistics, *Juggling Time: How Australian Families Use Time*, Office of the Status of Women, 1991.

Blackstone's Commentaries, Vol. 1.

Bottomley, Anne, Katherine Geive, Gay Moon and Angela Weir, *The Cohabitation Handbook*, Pluto Press, London, 1984.

Centre for Urban Research and Action, *'But I Wouldn't Want My Wife to Work Here': A study of migrant women in Melbourne industry*, Melbourne, 1976.

Dickens, Charles, *Oliver Twist*.

Finlay, H. A., *Family Law in Australia*, Butterworths, Sydney, 1978.

Ford, H. A. J. and W. A. Lee, *Principles of the Law of Trusts*, Law Book Co., 1983.

Gage, M. J., *Woman, Church & State*, Persephone Press, Massachusetts, 1980.

Green, Lisa, 'Bound by Law', *Elle*, April 1994.

Harrison, Margaret, *Australian Family Briefings No. 2*, Australian Institute of Family Studies, 1993.

Johnson, Elizabeth Ritchies, 'I Couldn't Afford My Job', *Redbook*, April 1991.

McDonald, Peter (ed.), *Settling Up—Property and Income Distribution on Divorce in Australia*, Australian Institute of Family Studies, 1986.

Mackay, Hugh, *Reinventing Australia*, Angus & Robertson, Sydney, 1993.

Orth, Maureen, 'What's Love Got to Do With it?', *Vanity Fair*, August 1990.

Ross, Nathan, MD, *The Psychiatry of Writing a Will*, Charles C. Thomas, Springfield, Illinois, 1989.

Roth, T., *Babylonian Marriage Agreements, Seventh to the Third Centuries, B.C.*, Verlag, Butzon and Becker Kevelaer, Germany, 1989.

Russell, Alice, 'Don't be a Money Moron', *SHE*, April 1994.

Sachs, Albie and Joan Hoff Wilson, *Sexuality and the Law*, Martin Robertson, Oxford, 1978.

Scutt, Jocelynne, *Women and the Law*, The Law Book Co., Sydney, 1990.

Shelton, Beth Ann, 'The Distribution of Household Tasks: Does a Wife's Employment Make a Difference?', *Journal of Family Issues*, Vol. 11, June 1990.

Social Welfare Research Centre, *Australian Women and Economic Security*, University of New South Wales, Sydney, 1988.

Somerset, Lady Anne, 'Elizabeth 1', *Connoisseur*, November 1991.

Spender, Lynne (ed.), *The Law Handbook*, 4th edn, Redfern Legal Publishing, Sydney, 1991.

Stern, Fritz, *Gold and Iron*, Alfred A. Knopf, New York, 1977.

HELPFUL RESOURCES

Applying for a Divorce: A Practical Guide to Processing Your Own Divorce, available from any Registry of the Australian Family Court.

In Love and Law (video), three case studies, available from any Registry of the Australian Family Court.

Spender, Lynne (ed.), *The Law Handbook*, 4th edn, Redfern Legal Centre Publishing, Sydney, 1991.

Women's Legal Resources Centre, *Law and Relationships: a woman's A–Z guide*, Redfern Legal Centre Publishing, Sydney, 1992.

INDEX

A

age pension, 119, 122
assets, 42, 158
   pooled, 30
   hidden, 104, 118
Attwood, Margaret, 161
Australian Bureau of Statistics, 11, 127
Australian Institute of Family Studies, 11, 44

B

bankruptcy, 84
Bernard, Jessie, 7
Brown, Marion, 25, 26
business assets, 96
   men's alienation of, 96
business records, 105

C

care of parents, 8
carer's pension, 131
cash flow statement, 37–40
charge account, 43
cheque account, 15, 31, 44
children, 6, 7, 98, 121
   loans to, 159
children's rights, 162–5

LYNNE SPENDER is variously a writer, editor, lecturer (working mainly in the areas relating to women and the law), critic, social commentator, lawyer, mother and teacher – although not necessarily in this order. She is currently employed as Executive Officer of the Australian Society of Authors. This is her fourth book.

SHELBY WHITE is a financial journalist who has written and lecturered on the subject of money. Her articles have appeared in many publications including *Forbes*, *Barron's*, *The New York times*, *Institutional Investor* and *Corporate Finance*.